The Secret History
of the
Reptilians

THE

SECRET

HISTORY

OF THE

REPTILIANS

The Pervasive

Presence of

the Serpent

in Human

History,

Religion, and

Alien Mythos

Scott Alan Roberts

NEW PAGE BOOKS
A division of The Career Press, Inc.
Pompton Plains, NJ

THE SECRET HISTORY OF THE REPTILIANS
EDITED BY JODI BRANDON
TYPESET BY EILEEN MUNSON
Cover design by Scott Alan Roberts
Printed in the U.S.A.

To order this title, please call toll-free 1-800-CAREER-1 (NJ and Canada: 201-848-0310) to order using VISA or MasterCard, or for further information on books from Career Press.

CAREER PRESS

New Page BOOKS

The Career Press, Inc.
220 West Parkway, Unit 12
Pompton Plains, NJ 07444
www.careerpress.com
www.newpagebooks.com

Library of Congress Cataloging-in-Publication Data
Roberts, Scott Alan.
   The secret history of the reptilians : the pervasive presence of the serpent in human history, religion, and alien mythos / by Scott Alan Roberts.
      p. cm.
   Includes bibliographical references and index.
   ISBN 978-1-60163-251-7 -- ISBN 978-1-60163-542-6 (ebook)
1. Serpents--Folklore. 2. Serpents--Mythology. 3. Serpents--Religious aspects. 4. Civilization, Ancient--Extraterrestrial influences. I. Title.

   GR740.R65 2013
   398.24'52796--dc23

                                                              2012039161

*D*edication

For better, for worse;
For richer, for poorer;
In faith, in cognitive dissonance;
When writing, when facing writer's block…

Although these were not the vows of our nuptial bliss, my wife, Raini, has been the experiencer, in and throughout, hefting all of these things as they blethered and bilged from me, although not all occurred during the particular writing of this particular book.

For all the months of time I spent researching, reading, writing, rewriting, lying in bed with my laptop casting a blue-gray luminescence about our room in the middle of the night; for all the times I excitedly distracted her from her tasks or—even worse, her slumber—to read new translations of ancient Sumerian cuneiforms or newly stumbled upon historical information that prodded me from my intellectual bienséance; for all the times she was over-burdened with being the single parent—the war widow—of our two wonderful, little children, Flynn and Rhowan Claire, and my 11-year-old son, Samuel, while I was off campaigning through ancient texts and pop cultural fantasies—all the while remaining grounded and supportive despite her frustrations with my brooding creativity, and uplifting during her motherly vehemence.

For providing an atmosphere where I could work and think and create, while taking on the heavier burden of wrangling the pre-teen, the toddler, and the babe, doing her best to keep the extraneous daily affairs of the household off my plate so I could write; for bringing me coffee and sitting on my lap to hear me read things that I am sure either bored her to tears, or during which she could have been engaging in something much more aligned to her own schedule, likes and agenda for those times, I loving dedicate this book to my wonderful, caring, supportive wife, **Raini Roberts.** This book is as much a product of her stalwart love and affection for me as it is the work of my own hand.

This book is also dedicated to the memory of Philip Coppens, whose life and research has been an inspiring, integral part of who I am. Go rest high on that mountain, my dear friend.

Acknowledgments

When there are so many books available on the shelves, it must seem a small thing to the common reader that an author of just one small book could spend any amount of significant time or space acknowledging the people who helped along the way. But it truly is not any small task, nor is it anything even close to insignificant. Without these people I am about to mention, this book would not be a reality.

First I want to thank everyone at New Page Books who has had a hand in publishing this work. Michael Pye, Laurie Pye, and Kirsten Dalley have been overtly supportive and unflinching proponents of my writing, and for that I cannot say enough how thankful I am. To Kirsten, especially, I want to say thank you for putting up with my inane schedule, and for tolerating my making you hound me for permissions and other details toward the end of this process. Thank you all for letting me part of what you are at New Page Books.

To my wife, Raini Roberts, I want to say thank you for putting up with my distractedness and downright surliness while I, sometimes literally, paced the floors and remained in an agitated, unruly state while contemplating what I hope translates into the struggle of dealing with some of the issues in this book. This isn't all just folly to me, but highly representative of fundamental, foundational changes in my beliefs and intellectual approaches to things I once thought so substantial. Thank you, Raini.

To my dearest of friends, my brother, my cohort in *Intrepid Magazine* and *Paradigm Symposium*, my ally and fellow explorer, Micah Hanks, I cannot express how thankful I am to have you in my life. Your help in constructing elements of this book are astronomically off the scale, and were it not for your consistent uplifting nature, and your research and work on my behalf, this book would most certainly not exist in the form it is in today. I love you with all my heart, my dear friend, and may the gods place your essence in the heavens for your care and selfless nature. Thank you for "making it so," oh, Science Officer.

Once again I must thank my old friend and professor Dr. Charles Aling, for it was he who originally sparked in me a love of history and archaeology. Although he and I may reside on differing sides of the theo-historical fence in some regards, he remains an inspiration whose influence has deep roots in who and what I have become. Perhaps we can sit over coffee and you can take me to task for some of my ideas and interpretations, and push me to continually do better, as you have always done.

Father Jack Ashcraft, thank you for listening. Thank you for inspiring and prodding me to think. You have been a good friend, indeed, and without your valuable influence in my life, I would be a poorer, sadder man. You have heard my caterwauls, misgivings, frustrations, dismissive pangs, and struggles of faith. Thank you for being not just an ear, but a dear friend through the process of writing this book.

Anthony F. Sanchez, you are someone who has established yourself as a dear friend, and your writing and conversations and ever-present encouragements are things of beauty to me. Thank you.

Dr. John Ward, thank you for your historical and archaeological input. Your invaluable information on the Thule and the 19th-century influences, though not all used in this book, established an incredible foundation from which to structure what did appear in these pages. As with *Nephilim*, we don't always see eye-to-eye on all these issues of interpretable history, but we do share a common love of the knowledge that comes from the research. I thank you for always being there for my questions and conversations. Your help in structuring parts of this book have immeasurable value. Thanks for the smokes and coffee by the Nile during our many video chats.

Thank you, Philip Coppens, for your wonderful Foreword and for your support in so many of my endeavors.

And for all those of you who let me rant and bounce ideas off your brains and hearts, I thank you unabashedly: Dave Potter, James Keuhl, Jim Fitzsimons, Barry Fitzgerald, Cassidy O'Connor-Nicholas, April Slaughter, Jane Scott (Mom), and many others far too numerous to list here.

And, of course, only last on the list due to her utter importance and influence, my dear friend on whom I cannot heap enough accolades and heartfelt praise and thanks—the inimitable, incomparable, amazing Marie D. Jones. You have been a dear friend, supporter, sounding board, and inspiration. Without your influence and prodding, this book—and the one before it—would not even exist. Thank you, my friend.

Contents

PART III:
The Serpent's Bloodline

Foreword

I remember ordering and reading Rene Andrew Boulay's *Flying Serpents and Dragons* from an alternative science mail order catalog in 1991. Boulay continued the work of American author Zecharia Sitchin, who had proposed that in our distant past, we were visited by beings from a 12th planet—allegedly named NIBIRU, the Crossing—in our solar system, who were the founders of most civilizations, but specifically that of Ancient Sumer. Whereas Sitchin had left the nature of these beings blank, Boulay claimed that these beings were reptilian. Boulay argued that there were numerous references in ancient accounts, including the Bible, that showed that some of our ancestors, including Noah, still showed physical marks of their reptilian origins, as we were a genetic manipulation of Earthly humanoids and Nibirian reptilians.

The early 1990s was also the time when thousands of mostly Americans were reporting "UFO abductions." Some of these abductors were described as reptilian entities. These two ingredients were mixed by British conspiracy author David Icke, who proclaimed that the British Queen Elizabeth II was actually a reptilian in disguise—a gimmick that guaranteed his claims would make headline news, including the British tabloids who loved that a former BBC sports presenter had made such outrageous claims. In fact, his claim was very much on par with what could be seen in the 1980s popular science fiction television series *V*, which portrayed a reptilian alien species that colonized Earth.

The theme that there are reptilian overlords overseeing the fate of humanity is a strong presence in modern conspiracy literature. As I appear on the popular television show *Ancient Aliens* and people as a consequence assume I have editorial input, one of the most frequently asked question is whether there is going to be a special on the Annunaki, the name the conspiracy-minded Sitchinites have given to our assumed reptilian overlords.

Of course, our current mindset didn't begin with David Icke; he merely played with an archetype that is far older and perpetually remained popular. The source of all evil in the Bible has become commonly identified as a reptilian being—a serpent. Though the crime the serpent seems to commit in the Bible is quite minor—providing information to Adam and Eve—as Christianity grew in popularity and power, it sought to personalize evil in the form of Lucifer and the devil, who became identified with that speaking serpent of the Garden of Eden.

If the devil is one of your most prominent identifiers, it is not surprising that serpents face an uphill struggle in popularity contests, though this is a cultural phenomenon. In the New World, the Feathered Serpent Quetzalcoatl was seen as a culture bringer, while the Vision Serpent helped the Mayan king in receiving information from the underworld. Though it shows that serpents were not always seen as evil, it does show, even in the biblical account, that intelligent serpents have provided our ancestors with knowledge, including otherworldly knowledge.

With a topic that has been identified by the Church for almost two millennia as the root of all evil, wading through the material is not a simple task. Sitchin and Icke are but two of a long list of researchers who have stranded in the murky waters of the reptilian archetype. Scott

Roberts fortunately boldly goes where few men have surfaced from, providing a well-balanced, innovative, and insightful approach to the topic.

It is time to become reacquainted with our reptilian neighbor, who seems to have a consistent, cross-cultural reputation of bringing us knowledge. It is high time we learn....

Philip Coppens

August 8, 2012

Preface

"Mankind is poised midway between the gods and the beasts."

—Plotinus

Writing a book about the ever-enigmatic race of extraterrestrial Reptilians is as simplistic a task as writing a book about the divinity of the historical Jesus. Fluxing in and out between myth and science, history and religion, all tempered with a healthy dose of "show-me-the-facts" skepticism, the very notion could drive one to the hard conclusion that establishing fact beyond a shadow of a doubt is nearly impossible in its efforts. The implications of the comparative historical and religious touch points are so far-reaching that the meanderings of myth one must follow to seek efficacious tendrils of fact could most certainly drive one mad in its contemplation.

What is it that religion and science aren't telling me about where I come from and why I am here? And why is the Serpent, a being both feared and revered, so inextricably linked to the misty imaginations and fortified spiritualities of man?

When I was a kid, I was deathly afraid of the dark.

Back then, I had a newspaper delivery route that encompassed several city blocks around my neighborhood in the farthest reaches of northern Minneapolis, slipping over into the closest residential areas along the busy middle-class suburb on the west bank of the Mississippi River. As a paperboy, it was my after-school responsibility to ensure that the people on my route received their copy of the *Minneapolis Star* every afternoon, before the dinner hour. That was the easy part of my job, which earned me about $8 per week. (In 1970, that was big money for a school kid.)

The hard part of my job was the Sunday morning route. The Sunday paper was three times as thick as the daily paper, and required me to rise at about 3 a.m., head to the paper shack (the pick-up location in our district, located about six blocks from my house), and collate the several sections of the paper for my route. I would then load those papers into my large, metal, bright yellow, two-wheeled cart, as they were far too thick and cumbersome to carry in my canvas sack.

Our house sat on a corner lot, and, despite the yellowish street lamp at the apex of the two bordering streets, our yard was always completely engulfed in the black shadows of night when I'd rise to walk to the paper shack. I remember standing there on the back cement steps of the house, jumping down into the dark yard and grabbing for the yellow handle of my paper cart. I'd yank it out of its spot and run, headlong through the yard to the dimly lit street. While standing beneath the incandescent glow, which created a 12-foot circle of safety around me, I would stare down the vacant, dead-of-night street to the next lamp, contemplating my sprint through the darkness between. Sucking up all my courage, gripping my yellow, two-wheeled anchor behind me, I'd again close my eyes tightly and run with all my might toward the next streetlamp, squinting only momentarily to make sure I hadn't deviated off my course and into the shadows that lined the street.

I would repeat this blind feat at every corner until I finally reached the safety of the corrugated tin shack, which was usually already bustling with other kids loading their paper carts.

I don't know what it was that created such a fear of the dark for me. Perhaps it was many hours watching *Dark Shadows,* a show filled with vampires, werewolves, and ghosts that scared the beejeebies out of me. Or maybe it was the thought of aliens and monsters that would spring from the bushes and devour my guts while I was still alive, kicking and screaming. Then again, it may have been all of those things simply combined with my innate fear of the unknown—that sense we all have that makes you tingle when you enter a dark room or pass a shadowy alcove that you absolutely know—beyond a shadow of a doubt—is inhabited by some otherworldly, carnivorous entity. The unknown has always been the primordial slime of the imagination, the place where we birth and foster our most terrifying nightmares.

My boyhood friend and fellow paperboy Doug Beman and I would, on many Sunday mornings, lay atop the newspapers stacked in our respective carts, and philosophize—as only fifth graders can do—beneath a corner street lamp, waiting for the earliest sliver of silvery-blue on the eastern horizon. There was one pre-dawn morning when we watched a cat slowly cross the road about 50 feet away from us, and we mused whether or not God had taken the form of that cat to come and watch over us. We took that reasoning and mused even further, reflecting on all the different things that had happened to us in our sphere of existence that might have conjured such a theophany (although we didn't use those particular words, as they were far outside our 10-year-old lexicon). As we sat there talking, we looked at each other and were astonished to see we were both shedding tears—not of sadness or any sort of uncontrollable weeping, but from something that hit very close to home in our psyches, on a very deep, subconscious level. And it was from that point we determined that God or his angels truly existed and could manifest before us in any shape or form they desired. And the cat, from that day forward, became the object of our fecund, private, little religion.

I imagine, now, some 40 years later, that this could be very much like the experiences of the ancients, when they sat philosophizing beneath flickering nocturnal torchlight, gazing up at the sky, only to be interrupted by some astronomical phenomena or the unexplained, unrecognized rustling of something out there in the dark, prompting the same sort of musings my friend and I experienced several thousand years in their future.

What was their religious cat, I wonder? Who or what became the object that, for them, could so capture their worship in the midst of their contemplative brooding? What was it that caused them to conceive deities and imagine giants from the dark to such a degree that they would soon end up etched for all time on the local cliff face, painted with dye concocted from the roots of the plants that grew around their village?

Or perhaps their ancient encounters were far more tangible: men from faraway tribes appearing in their village for the very first time— beings from the desert, hills, skies, and possibly even the stars. And from these encounters were birthed their oral stories that were generations growing into legends and myths.

On the heels of *The Rise and Fall of the Nephilim*, which examined and explored evidences and theological, anthropological, and comparative cultural accounts that the human race was visited in ancient times by non-human intelligences that interrupted and influenced the development of humanity, these pages will take the case another step further. There is a lot of mythos out there to suggest that we have been visited by "extraterrestrial" intelligences, so much so that it has permeated our popular culture, our intellectual dialogues, and even our religions and spiritualities. In fact, there exists more "evidence" to support the existence of UFOs than there is to support the existence of God—and seeing as God never really seems too overtly interested in proving himself beyond the heartfelt acceptance of the faithful, that is a fairly concise statement.

Notions of beings from outside this world impregnating humans are as old as humanity itself, up to this current day. And those histories and accounts have comprised a bulk of human mythology, legend, religion, and superstition. But what if those ancient visitations and encounters with non-human intelligences were far less than the stuff of "first contact"? What if those races manipulated the DNA of homo sapiens, creating a "slave race" to do the bidding and work of Reptilian-hominid overlords?

The theory of ancient alien interruption and the possibility of extraterrestrial reptilian races is not a new one, and its purveyors have been writing and theorizing on the topic for decades. Ever since early humans first gazed up in wonder at the star-blanketed night sky, we were intrigued by the seemingly unanswered questions of a mysterious, unattainable universe intrigued by its unexplained mysteries. Early mythologies and legends give the circumstantial evidences of mysterious objects roaring across the heavens. Shards of ancient tablets and shreds of ancient documents describe phenomenal, unexplained manifestations in the skies, and virtually every culture and religion relates visitations from angels, demons, devils, and gods who visited mankind in ancient times. And humanity, in its infancy, described these visitations from the sky in the only terms they could understand. Of course they were deities.

Despite this decades-old—if not centuries-old—debate, there is still a lot of disinformation and misinformation out there that begins with an atheistic point of view bent on disproving the religious and spiritual elements of creation and otherworldly interaction, as well as the opposite, which would seek to disprove or naysay anything that smacks of anything outside the box of established traditional theology.

Despite being a secular society, focused on the tangibles of day-to-day material safety nets and a laissez-faire adherence to entrenched generational religious denominations, people have an underlying draw to old spiritualities and covert superstitions. Though outwardly displaying a dismissive attitude toward anything that smacks of a deeper connection with traditional beliefs and spiritual roots, usually accompanied by an almost-apologetic acquiescence to having grown up in a faith or religion, the overt façade belies a deeper, inextricable-yet-unrequited draw to theo-philosophical questions, mixed with a fascination of God, UFOs, ghosts, angels, demons, and everything in between. As for scientific dogma, most people dismiss the sciences as "mathematical things" that are either too heady or too emotionally dissociative to matter, and far less things to incorporate into any sort of daily life, and they tend to ignore them altogether. Unless Morgan Freeman narrates a show about the universe or genetics, science has become a thing that has been relegated to the realm of geeks, nerds, and academia. Why, you'd never find a scientist drinking beer, eating hot dogs, changing diapers, and belching out his new theory on the Higgs Boson…right?

When you strip away all the externals and lay bare the hearts of most people, at the core is their need to know who they are, where they came from, why they exist, and what the hell else is out there—regardless of how much they try to make the rest of the world believe they view these things as unimportant. Myth, legend, theology, and meta-science comprise the underlying faiths and beliefs of most Americans, who would otherwise give no outward indication that they hold to such values, even on a level of simple curiosity.

This book represents the *never-ending-book*, contained in 220 or so pages. You'll find yourself, at times, deeply entrenched in facts and details, sorting through historical and linguistic material, but I have presented in such a way that is, hopefully, exciting and enlightening while riddled with bits and pieces of humor and my own anecdotal rants. In other places, you will endure my pedagogic philosophizing mixed with my middle-of-the-road positioning while attempting to bring a clear connection between myth and anthropology. In these pages we will discuss and hopefully provoke thought, addressing the innate need we all have to know the answers to these age-old questions via a very focused examination of a race of beings who visited earth, millennia past, for the sole purpose of not simply cohabiting, but creating and manipulating a race of underlings.

Utilizing a scholarly approach, blended with a bit of light-hearted tongue-in-cheek intellectualism, I will engage, on a deeper level, the examination of familiar accounts in the Old Testament book of Genesis, combined with similar, corresponding accounts in various other cultures, religions, and spiritualities, cracking wide open the theories of extraterrestrial interruption and intercourse with early humanity, thus challenging and bringing new light to what we have discarded as mere mythology and ufological "urban myth."

What if non-human intelligences bequeathed a race of mixed-blood humans?

This book explores the cross-cultural theological accounts as well as the current New Age movements that capitalize on fear mongering, the Illuminati, and the behind-the-scenes of the behind-the-scenes of what is taking place in humanity. We will explore the Merovingian bloodlines, the bloodlines of the Nephilim, and the presence of Reptilian and other alien races working to destroy, aid, and/or bolster humankind, all as they precariously balance against ancient religious mythology of the presence of the serpent in and throughout ancient history and religions.

The Rise and Fall of the Nephilim established that something huge happened to the human race in our ancient past, supported by the comparative religions, cultures, and archaeology of the world. Utilizing archaeological record, anthropological studies, and comparative religious examinations, we dig even deeper to establish what is already so evident yet hidden and encoded in the world today.

It's a grossly huge topic that deserves an equally huge scholarly look and treatment. That does not mean we will, in these pages, be able to exhaustively cover all the angles and bring conclusive answers to every issue. But these pages will establish a great place to start looking at the questions from a new vantage.

I am told that people want to know precisely where you stand on an issue when you present it in a book such as this. What you will find from me is someone who straddles the fence between science and faith, mythology and archaeology, legend and history. They all work together to bring us a clearer understanding of what exists out there. You simply cannot have one without the other—and this is the fallacy of discarding one for the other, because, as I have contended time and time again, there are veils that simply cannot be pierced, and eschewing the unquantifiable, although scientifically acceptable, is philosophically irresponsible.

> "There is nothing truer than myth: history, in its attempt to realize myth, distorts it, stops halfway; when history claims to have succeeded, this is nothing but humbug and mystification. Everything we dream is realizable. Reality does not have to be: it is simply what it is."
>
> —Eugene Ionesco

Introduction

"Snakes. Why'd it have to be snakes?"

—Indiana Jones

Every night a snake-like man would visit me in my house. I don't know how he got in or where he came from. He was just there, standing more than 6 feet tall, with smooth, delicately scaled, greenish-brown skin, almost silky to the touch, giving me the sense of a cobra or some other sort of sleek reptile. His eyes were large and glossy black with vertical iris slits that glinted an iridescent yellow. When he spoke, his voice was as deep and hollow as a bottomless canyon, rapacious and seductive all at once. His breath held a faint scent of cinnamon. He said he was from another part of the galaxy, somewhere in Orion's Belt, and that I had been someone "They" had been watching for a long, long time....

That is the beginning of a story told to me, several years ago, by a woman whose name I have long since forgotten. She went on to describe a fearsome yet benevolent creature who described himself to her as being part of a hostile race set on the destruction of humanity—a course that was determined long, long ago in humanity's primordial past. This woman even sent me drawings she had done of this being, as well as much more descriptive, and at times quite sexual, narrative.

They, too, have simply vanished along the way, more a result of my own ramshackle filing system than any sort of weird conspiracy theory.

Her story, along with many other similar accounts of such beings I have heard throughout the years, was relegated to the back of my brain, filed under: "Interesting but Nutty." There it sat in a metaphoric mental stew pot, slowly simmering—a reptilian "stone soup" growing in richness and flavor as I subconsciously added the bits of ingredients delivered by all sorts of characters and sources along the way. Every so often the lid of the pot would rattle, releasing a steamy, fragrant aroma of hearty broth, bringing me back to the awareness that I had something cooking over there in the kitchen of my mind. And what was cooking was a splendid, blended concoction of theology, archaeology, ufology, psychology, cosmology, anthropology, and every other little "ology" in between.

Having recently completed my work on the *The Rise and Fall of the Nephilim*, I found myself in a highly agitated state of spiritual and emotional unrest. I had either just opened up (at least for me) an exponentially expanded view of who God is, or I had, in essence, eliminated his existence altogether. Either the god of the Hebrew and Christian scriptures existed as I had been taught in cloistered, fundamentalist academia, or I had effectively stripped away his divinity by lowering him a few rungs on the ladder to the level of non-human entity with some power over the human race to create, procreate, and destroy. To me, this represented a crisis of faith, and I entered the grieving process of the "loss of innocence," as embodied in the theology I once adhered to so strictly and believed in so intimately. When my theology was forced to stand against the onslaught of history, comparative religion, cumulative cultural mythologies, and archaeological record, everything about my religious practice seemed to be ripped open and lain bare, as if by a great whirlwind. And all that was left was a naked faith, shivering in the harsh cold of a veritable nuclear winter of pragmatic thinking and common sense, void the protective cloak of religious insulation.

The Serpent in the Garden of Eden took on the completely different role of historical influence once I was able to view the story without the filter of religion or denominational interpretation. When I was able to see that this creature, as described in the Hebrew Bible's Book of Genesis, was similar to if not synonymous with many other cultural tales of trickster beings who brought knowledge and illumination to early humans, I saw a much bigger picture encoded within those pages of biblical scripture. When people step outside the box of religion and denominational spirituality, they find themselves in a unique vantage point of being able to see myriad varied tales that have intrinsic common threads woven throughout.

It's rather like walking into one of those glorious, old theatres that dominated the cultural avenues of upper-crust society at the turn of the last century. As you entered the theatre and walked down the main aisle, the gilded proscenium and glittering chandeliers sparkled the magnificence of the thespian palace, built as a showcase for the art of the show. And there, lining the aisles were row after row of plush velvet seats, all identical and all capable of holding the weight of a patron every night. Yet despite their identical construct and appearance, each chair held a different perspective of the show being performed on the stage. Depending on which seat you settled into, your viewpoint of what was being performed up front varied. Some seats were side-by-side, so their vantage was nearly identical; other seats delivered views from the far sides, back, or distant last row of the balcony. Some seats even had partially obstructed views. But in a literal, mathematical sense, not a single seat held the same exact vantage point or view of the show being played out onstage. But one thing was also sure: No matter where you sat in that theatre, and no matter which vantage point from which you viewed the show, the performance was unaltered.

Perception does not alter reality; it merely alters practice. The show on stage doesn't change dependent on where I am sitting or from what vantage point I am viewing. Only my perception of it alters. So the trick is to not be part of the audience, but rather a part of the play—a member of the cast. A participant, as opposed to an observer.

The Hebrew story of a race interrupted is an encoded one: Adam and Eve, the Serpent, their offspring, the fallen state of humanity, and the proclamation of an angry deity. These are all elements of an encoded cover story, as I spoke about extensively in both *The Rise and Fall of the Nephilim* and in *Lost Civilizations and Secrets of the Past*. There is a much bigger message than the meticulously buried messages of the biblical tales that is similar in tone and thread to hundreds of other cultural religious mythologies of spectacular non-human beings interacting with the human race of ancient times. Common to nearly all of these cultural stories is the common thread of residual bloodlines that run through the course of all of human history.

Call it religious mumbo-jumbo, or theological manipulation. Look at it as the establishment of the messianic bloodlines and the mixed race meant to thwart the coming of the Kinsman Redeemer. But no matter how you view it, the story of the ongoing bloodlines remain a concurrent theme, from the very first utterance of an enmity that will exist between the seed of the serpent and the seed of the woman, all the way down the historical biblical genealogies that are there within Old Testament passages to exhort the ever present, vigilant eye to be ever watchful of the *pure human line* versus the oppositional mixed-blood lineage.

Humanity was visited by non-human entities that from the very beginning introduced an alternate bloodline that has carried all the way down the historical record to current day—the bloodline of the serpent. But we only see fragmentary bits and pieces, rather like a checkerboard where half the spaces are occupied, but the other half remain completely void and empty.

I am not one who quickly sidles up alongside "great awakenings," new spiritual movements, or hyper-fastidious conspiracy theories. They all generally tend, to me, to be the stuff of manufactured emotional reactions to hypothesis that are either not well researched—historically, spiritually, anthropologically—and many times are not well-articulated, despite their complex yet imaginative constructs. Most of these types of theoretical movements rely far too heavily on fanciful whimsy, bolstered by a desire to find something new and exciting, filled with elements unwittingly designed to "suspend reality," or move the mind away from the mundane—not to mention the targeting of political opponents.

Far too many times throughout human history we have seen the devastatingly horrific result of revolutionary new movements that explode onto the scene, spewing theoretical spiritualities, political conspiracies or *vox populi, vox Dei,* but in the long run end up being little more than mere flashes in the pan, lacking substance and longevity, resulting in the martyrdom (whether literal or metaphoric) of self-proclaimed messiahs and the murder, suicide, or disbanding of disciples. Yet those movements that do gain a foothold and garner mass followings trend to the darker elements of racial bigotry, genocide, political xenocide, and holocaust, building gravitas and momentum by catering to the fears of potential devotees and zealous followers alike.

People are always looking for something that is different than what they already have, or more exciting than what are told they should be satisfied with. Spiritually, politically, and conspiratorially based movements generally thrive within, around, and despite the well-established religions, spiritualities, sciences, and governments that are deeply entrenched in our societies and cultural histories.

On the flip side of the coin, deep within well-established philosophies, religions, and political mindsets, there are embedded messages and encoded languages that tend to shift the paradigm away from the established way of thinking. Once this new information is articulated and disseminated, established systems of spiritual belief and practice are enhanced, are expanded, and in many cases rewrite the history of a well-established, firmly entrenched philosophy. The end result is that the new twist can sometimes appear to be a new awakening or new conspiracy theory, when it is in reality an illumination of something that already exists—an expansion based on a fresher understanding of what was already there.

The Serpent in the Garden of Eden, though allegorical in nature and very possibly the stuff of Hebrew religious mythology, is a figure that represents a very real source of what has become an emerging understanding of a very real bloodline running through the veins of human descendents throughout all of human history.

There is, indeed, a Reptilian factor to humanity, and it shines through our religious and cultural icons. The serpent is one of the oldest and most widespread mythological symbols. Snakes have been associated with some of the oldest religious rituals known to humankind and have carried the dual expression of both good and evil. From the Hebrews' Serpent in the Garden to the Mayans' Quetzalcoatl; the Bhuddist Naga to the rattlesnake on the early Colonial American flags; the African Dahomey and Aido Hweido to Jörmungandr of the Nordic mythologies; and Ouroboros, the ancient Near Eastern serpent devouring its own tail representing the great cycle of life. Then there exist everything from sea serpents to St. George and the Dragon, and even the medical caduceus.

If symbolism, however, was all there was to the traceable bloodlines of the serpent, the flesh and blood of the story would be a short, sweet, picturesque history lesson. Demystifying the cover story of the serpent in the Garden is only the beginning. Identifying the source point of his and countless other mythological and cultural counterparts is what will allow us to see the tangible evidence of ancient human encounters with non-human entities, revealing what that lies beneath the surface of old mythologies as they meld into current-day accounts.

The human race has not yet experienced a full-fledged "first contact" with any alien race—at least none that has been disclosed. Those who have made experiential disclosures are generally pooh-poohed by the skeptical, scientific, religious, and even hopeful, believing camps. We do have, however, countless numbers of ancient documents and texts that record interactions with what can only be described as non-human intelligences. Most of these ancient documents categorize these intelligences as their version of gods, angels, demons, and spirit beings—the biblical stories of the Sons of God, the Watchers, and their offspring, the Nephilim being prime examples.

One of the criticisms thrown at most religious documents is that they cannot be trusted as quantifiable historical sources, because they are books of faith. The Bible falls under this sweeping dismissal all the time. However, most ancient historical documents were synonymous with religious texts, as ancient peoples did not separate those two driving forces of civilization the way we do in modern affairs. Even as recently as the reigns of Henry VIII and Elizabeth I of England, many royal proclamations were linked to the religious views of the monarchs, and in that period of history in England, the conflict between Catholicism and Protestantism was a driving force. Keeping this non-separation of powers squarely in mind, note that Reptilian creatures have filled the texts of ancient documents. To cite just a small handful:

+ The serpent Nachash interacted with and impregnated Eve in the Garden of Eden story.

+ Oannes, the half-fish/half-man, and his people rose up out of the Persian Gulf to teach civilization to the ancient Mesopotamians.

+ The Cannanite goddess Qetesh interacted with serpent beings.

- In Sumerian literature, Gilgamesh loses his powers of immortality to a serpent.

- The Sumerian fertility god, Ningizzida, is depicted as a serpent.

- The ancient Jewish (Hebrew) tribe of Levi is said to have conquered Europe under a surge driven by Reptilian "illuminati-like" overlords

- Ho Ti, of the House of Sui, also known as the Serpent Emperor of China (618 AD) found a wounded serpent and nursed it to health, after which it returned to him with a reward of recompense.

And there is much more, as we will discover throughout these pages.

The serpent has been a pervasive presence indeed throughout human history, filling our religious scriptures, historical tomes, and mythological tales, and appearing on the faces of thousands of archaeological relics. And, yes, our theories of UFO visitations and extraterrestrial encounters have a decisive Reptilian influence in and throughout the ancient alien subculture. Simply enter the word *reptilian* in an Internet search engine and you will find millions of entries, ranging from the profusely inane and undocumented to highly politicized pseudo-religious movements, to loosely documented claims by highly credible people.

The opening lines of this book began by recounting an experiencer's tale of interaction with a single member of an "alien" reptoid race. We will now move forward to explore the veracity of these experiential claims, as well as the serpent as a religious symbol, a political force, a mythological influence, and a race of both intraterrestrial and extraterrestrial races bent on the mutual destruction and salvation of our species.

The Empire
of the
Serpent

PART I

Chapter One

The Annunaki and Their Sumerians

"[The realm of myth and magic] is a dangerous field:
fairies abound, good fairies and bad fairies, dragons and
dragon-slayers, gods and goddesses, truth and untruth,
history and legend, science and fiction, inextricably
mixed and fused. But what has archaeology to do with
it, you will say? Archaeology is concerned with bones
and flints, with pots and pans and post-holes, with
stone and metal, in short, with the material remains
and spades to dig them up with."

—F.J. Tritsch, "Myth, Magic and Archaeology"

Going back to the very beginning is generally the best place to travel
when looking for the roots of any mythology. It's in the fertile soil
of creation that we find the seeds that sprouted and grew into the massive, towering beanstalk that has led us to the realm of the giants and the
golden goose in the clouds. And whether allegorical, mythological, legendary, or the stuff of fable, there is generally always an incontrovertible
fact at the core—that thing that started the whole story. And let's make no
mistake about it: Once you start delving into the depths of comparative
ancient stories, their encoded similarities and subsequent decipherment,
you enter a muddled world of interpretation that will raise both dust
and ire. Clearing the air is the monumental task with which you are left.

There are mindsets that are at complete odds here, like two trains running at high speed toward each other on the same set of tracks. There is bound to be an eventual collision of catastrophic proportion—in this case, the repeating scenario of science colliding with belief and archaeology running headlong into myth (and vice versa). But there has to be an accounting on both parts. Faith and belief open themselves to upholding the sometimes-nonsensical, mystical, un-provable, capricious, and many times ambiguous, spiritual soul of religion and mythology, whereas science and archaeology will eschew—many times with great disdain—the unquantifiable as folly, rooting out what they define as fact from fiction, no matter how grounded in their own sense of objectivity and importance—rather like when the science of the day upheld that the earth was the center of the universe and the sun rotated around it. Those were simply the facts based on the available knowledge and interpretation, and they were religiously adhered to by the academia of the day—until, that is, science developed the capability to move beyond its limits and recalculate its positions, determining that the earth, indeed, rotated around the sun.

Now, bear with me as I work through laying a little background that will serve as the platform from which we will engage in an examination of the secret history of the Reptilians.

The Naked Truth

When I completed my work on *The Rise and Fall of the Nephilim*, I recall sitting back in my office chair and staring at the ceiling for a long, silent time. In those minutes I was contemplating what it was that I had just written. In all the research I did into the Book of Genesis, from both Christian and Rabbinic standpoints, I found myself drawing further and further away from the God of my youth. It was not a deliberate distancing, but after stepping outside the box and looking back in, I found that the God I had discovered in my youth was not the same God that seemed to materialize after taking a closer look at more than dogmatic systematic theology. The God I grew up knowing was one of holiness, of benevolence, and ultimately of eternal, sacrificial, propitiating, atoning love. His was a love that transcended everything and embraced me where I was, saving me from myself, and the horrors of an eternal existence void of His loving presence.

Perhaps this was simply a byproduct of my need to step "outside the box" in order to see things from as objective a point of view as possible. This seems to be the problem with a purely academic—or secular—examination of these things: When you distance yourself from the possibility of the weird, odd, spiritual, and mythological, you deliberately set yourself up to look beyond the wonder and the possibilities, to funneling all research through a sterile filter.

What is even more profound is to observe the distillation of research by secular scholarship and that the scientific and skeptical approach to biblically themed topics, such as the Nephilim, seems to operate under a preconceived notion that the Bible cannot be taken literally in any form, including its historicity. One critic of *The Rise and Fall of the Nephilim* stated that I erred simply by placing any veracity at all in the biblical record. However, it has been quantified time and time again that the Bible is quite irrefutably strong in its historical presentations, albeit at times vague, limited, and deliberately not forthcoming in detailed information, as the contextual themes inclusive of some historical data were meant to present a faith principle, rather than historical documentation. Therefore the historical information was sometimes sketchy, at best. Skeptical researchers, honest to their scholarship, are finding it increasingly more difficult to dispute the overwhelming archeological evidence for the historical accuracy of the biblical accounts. Any corroboration of biblical historical facts, however, does not by any means emphatically state that the faith story wrapped around these events is "truth," but it does lend to the veracity of the Bible as a historically accurate document, aside from the religious and spiritual aspects of Judaism and Christianity. Biblical accounts that include such things as listings of nations, historic personages, customary rituals, and colloquial practices have been verified by archeological evidence and anthropological research. Secular academecians who have corner-stoned careers on criticism of biblical history have many times found themselves humiliated by new discoveries that validate the biblical accounts they had previously deemed to be myth (academic embarrassment). Among these are such discoveries as the existence of the obscure Hittites, King David of Israel, Goliath of Gath, and Pontius Pilate, the praefect of Judea during the lifetime of Jesus of Nazareth. Nelson Glueck, noted 20th-century Jewish archeologist whose work in biblical archaeology led to the discovery of more than 1,500 ancient sites, put it this way: "It may be stated categorically that no archeological discovery has ever controverted a single biblical reference. Scores of archeological findings have been made which confirm in clear outline or in exact detail historical statements in the Bible."[1]

Not surprisingly—as some think of the biblical record as being inaccurate and rife with faith stories alone—when stacked up against non-biblical accounts of historical events, the scriptural narratives reveal unflinching veracity. In his 1919 collection of essays and other journal work, *A Scientific Investigation of the Old Testament*, R.D. Wilson, who was fluent in 45 ancient languages and dialects (inclusive of all the biblical languages of common etymological origin, such as Hebrew, Aramaic, Assyrian, Phoenician, Sumerian, Babylonian dialects, Ethiopic, as well as several Egyptian and Persian dialects), engaged in a meticulous analysis of 29 different monarchs from 10 different nations mentioned in Masoretic texts (the Old Testament). By way of comparative analysis, every one of these monarchs had corresponding archeological artifacts documented by secular historians containing their names, syllable-by-syllable, consonant-by-consonant. Wilson demonstrated that the monarchical names as recorded in the biblical record matched the findings of secular historians and archaeological artifacts, accurate in minute detail to the chronological order of the kings. Conversely, Wilson also demonstrated that many secular historical accounts were often filled with gross inaccuracies and were eventually deemed quite unreliable. Ptolemy, the famed Librarian of Alexandria, and even Herodotus were horrendously inaccurate in their documentation of royal names, and in many instances even misspelled the names (in the Library of Alexandria) to the point of nearly being unable to be recognized when compared to their respective archaeological artifacts or ancient monuments. Their research simply required more evidentiary research to establish any sort of accurate corroboration.

Even the well-known 19th-century archaeologist and historian Sir William Ramsay, a noted scholarly skeptic of biblical history, converted to Christianity after his travels to Asia Minor to conduct meticulous research and archaeological excavations into the New Testament's Gospel according to Luke and Luke's follow-up historical record, the Acts of the Apostles. The evidence Ramsay uncovered continually and incontrovertibly supported the historical record of the biblical writings of Luke. At a time when many secular historians and scholars dismissed the existence of most of Luke's record of governmental officials and geographical name-places, Ramsay's archeological digs actually flipped the naysayers' claims on their heads. Without error, Ramsey established through his excavations that Luke was accurate in naming countries, cities, islands, Roman officials, and many other salient details of historical record contained in the New Testament writings. As a result of his discoveries, Ramsay wrote: "I began with a mind unfavorable to it...but more recently I found myself brought into contact with the Book of Acts as an authority for the topography, antiquities, and society of Asia Minor. It was gradually borne upon me that in various details the (biblical) narrative showed marvelous truth."[2]

Ramsay also wrote: "Luke is a historian of the first rank; not merely are his statements of fact trustworthy...this author should be placed along with the very greatest historians."[3]

Although the previous paragraphs may have seemed a bit of a rabbit trail—for which I have become very well-known, as there is so much information that could be incorporated to illuminate any tidbit of information out there—I included them for the purpose of establishing the fact that not all religious literature is merely faith-based alone, despite many secular, skeptical opponents, in their own particular biases, wishing it were so. When you step outside the box of a particular faith, and look to find corroboration between historical data and scriptural teaching, using the faith writing as a guide, not a filter, you will find that biblical history, in particular, stands the test of historical scrutiny.

However, because the historical data may be reliable, this does not always necessitate the spiritual information it's housed within is universal truth. Though I can insist that the Constitution of the United States is a historical document and uphold it as closely as possible to its original intent, there will be others who interpret its words through different filters, thereby causing decades of debate on its veracity versus its interpretability. The same is true with religious writings.

On a spiritual level, my personal universe was very small back in the days of my youth, and God was a God, I was told, who waited for me with open arms, to take my troubled life and make it something beautiful through His saving, undeserved grace. Yet the older I got, and the more I dug into the topic of the biblical Nephilim, the more I found a God emerging from the murkiness that was, in nature and human-like emotional volatility, ultimately detached from humanity—a God who didn't give (and pardon my plain vernacular here) two shits about humanity. This is mythological interpretation as opposed to historical veracity, but it is the result of my spiritual studies and evolving understanding of the spiritual content of these ancient documents. Despite all the teaching about God and all the systematic theology in my Bible school and seminary days, the Elohim of the Old Testament seemed more concerned and focused on the stuffs going on in the realm of the heavens than he did with human beings. There are many instances in the Bible's stories of God's dealings with mankind where human life was as dispensable as yesterday's news, and several occasions where God insisted on their extermination and even followed through with it by divine judgment or mandates passed on to His followers. And once I discovered that the Elohim were a *plurality*—a pantheon, if you will—dominated by a superior member of their caste of gods, the one, singular, omniscient, omnipresent God of my upbringing took a decidedly rear seat in the family van. Although there were plenty of scriptures that were interpreted as God's presence, love, and interaction with people, there were even more that spoke to His ability to be as human and unjust as any earthly monarch establishing his jealous reign over his subjects, enacting the wiping out of non-believers and the genocide of whole peoples in His justified wrath. There was even an account in the Old Testament Book of Exodus where God was going to destroy His promised people, and it took the intervention of Moses to hold back God's wrath, reminding Him of His promise to Abraham and caused God to "repent of the evil he was going to do" (Exodus 32:14).

The Jewish Midrash teaches (Ecclesiastes 5:4) that "Three things annul evil decrees: 1) prayer; 2) charity [righteousness]; 3) repentance [tshuvah]." In striking contrast, however, in Bamidbar Rabbah (23:8; cf: Exodus 32:14) we read that Moses "came forward and *made God repent* (author's emphasis)." In this case, it was the intervention of a righteous human being that preceded prayer, righteousness, or *teshuvah* [תשובה] on the part of evil-doers. There are several instances in Hebrew scripture where men intervened and changed the mind of God; Moses, Abraham, and Jonah, in particular, seemingly all had the influence to reverse what can be understood as God's "evil inclination." In fact, Exodus 32:9–14 passage says:

> 9–10God said to Moses, "I look at this people—oh! what a stubborn, hard-headed people! Let me alone now, give my anger free reign to burst into flames and incinerate them. But I'll make a great nation out of you *instead* (author's emphasis)."
>
> 11–13Moses tried to calm his God down. He said, "Why, God, would you lose your temper with your people? Why, you brought them out of Egypt in a tremendous demonstration of power and strength. Why let the Egyptians say, 'He had it in for them—he brought them out so he could kill them in the mountains, wipe them right off the face of the Earth.' Stop your anger. Think twice about bringing evil against your people! Think of Abraham, Isaac, and Israel, your servants to whom you gave your word, telling them 'I will give you many children, as many as the stars in the sky, and I'll give this land to your children as their land forever.'"
>
> 14And God did think twice. He *decided not to do the evil* (author's emphasis) he had threatened against his people.

In short, there are several biblical instances in which God looked more and more like Zeus, Neptune, Elil, and the other superior reigning gods of mythology than He did a real, substantive heavenly father that was so presented throughout my life. God began to look no different than all the other "false" gods we learned about in comparative religions courses. He started to take on the traits and attributes of a god created by man for the purpose of rallying the troops or controlling the erstwhile yet sinful courses of common folk who needed to be reigned in and controlled.

Further, as I began the research into ancient religions for the purpose of this book, I found much of what I had believed by faith to be the only-one-true-religion, to be simply the stuffs of revitalized, rewritten, reworked—possibly even plagiarized—religions of thousands of years prior to the writing of the compiled books we refer to today as the Bible. When Moses penned the Pentateuch (the first five books of the Hebrew Bible and the Christian Old Testament) in and around 1400 BCE (I believe there is absolutely no reason to doubt that these books were, at least originally, authored by Moses, and that he indeed was a real, historical person, as established in the dating system set forth in my previous work[4]), it is very clear that Moses "borrowed" information from the earlier Sumerian and Akkadian religions, recorded in cuneiform 1,500–2,000 years earlier, sometime between 2500 and 2800 BCE. (**Author's Note:** In *The Rise and Fall of the Nephilim,* when stating that the date of the Sumerian civilization flourished around "4500–4800 BCE," I meant to say 2500–2800 BCE, but inadvertently stated the number of years from today, backward, rather the correct date. Ah, the things that can get missed even in your most meticulous editing!) The evolution and migration of humans from the Fertile Crescent region between the Tigris and Euphrates rivers south and west into the Canaanite region brought with it, also, the evolution and transformation of ancient religion. The Hebrews picked up on the name "El" and incorporated it into their religion—their own, homespun version of a superior god and the pantheon of the Sumerians. Elil became Elohim, El Eliyon, El Shaddai of the Hebrew religion, while Enki/Ea, the base word for Ywhw, became Yahweh, or Jehovah.

However, when discussing this very issue of etymology of ancient god-names, my friend and Byzantine Catholic priest Father Jack Ashcraft said to me in a personal conversation, "The word 'Allah' can be found in use in the Syrian Churches. The etymology isn't the issue. Muhammad merely used a common word in his tribe for deity. The issue is the character, will, and salvific history of the deity concerned. If they do not match, they cannot be the same deity."

When considering this anthropological migration of religion and its adaptation of cultural words and names, it is interesting to note that the name "Allah" was one of the pagan deities of the Quraish. As a youth, Muhammad, who later founded the Islamic religion, participated in the worship of the 360 pagan gods of the Kabah in Mecca, overseen by the Quraish tribe to which Muhammad belonged. As Muhammad grew up, he was influenced by Jewish and Christian monotheists who condemned the polytheism of the Kabah. At some point in Muhammad's life, he became convinced that polytheism was completely incompatible for a nationalistic-based religion and sought to reject the 360 pagan gods with which he had been raised.[5] Muhammad was converted to the concept of monotheism through the influence and teachings of Judaism and Christianity.[6] However, being a proud nationalistic Arab, he sought not to change his people's beliefs completely, but turned reformer and sought to reboot his native pagan religion rather than adopt a completely different belief system altogether, such as Christianity. As a result, Muhammad took the chief pagan god of the Kabah in Mecca (Hubal/Allah[7]) and chose him to be his new monotheistic god. This god was already considered the chief god among the other gods at the Kabah. Muhammad's strategy was simple: Rather than converting all the Arab people to the monotheism of Christianity, he merely banished the other 359 pagan gods and chose Hubal/Allah to be the one and only god, thus giving Islam "Allah." In a very real sense, Muhammad created Islam out of whole cloth for the purpose of solidifying Arabic nationalism under one god and one religion—much the same as Constantine with Christianity in the early 300s AD.

The last thing I wish to do is dissuade anyone from their personal faith or traditional beliefs. However, in saying that, it also must be recognized that even the most sacredly held names in our most holy beliefs have come from earlier sources. Civilization developed and migrated across the globe, and with that came the migration and evolution of religious thought. Just as the early Christian church dislocated pagan tribes and usurped their places of high worship, burning down their sacred groves only to erect chapels and cathedrals in their place, so did ancient humanity as they borrowed and transformed religion into newer modes of practice and objects of worship.

This train of thought, of course, represents what religious scholars would call a secular view. It eliminates the need for faith, and filters the history of humanity and the development of religion and religious stories through the strainer of archaeology and anthropology. Accordingly, evangelicals and staunch adherents to Judeo-Christian faith, as well as Islam and other dogmatic faiths, would view this migration of religion and evolution of language as nothing more than a secularized explanation for something they accept by faith. At best they would accept by faith that the secular view can be merged with the religious mythology. Insisting that the so-called secular left despises them, Evangelical Christians maintain that post-modernism has moved the secularists to abandon absolutism for the more comfortable, objective, relative definition of "truth": "Evangelical Christians believe...there is absolute truth which applies to all people, in all cultures, for all times. Evangelicals recognize that this objective and absolute truth is found ultimately in the one true God...and in His revelation given to us personally in Jesus Christ and in the Bible.[8]

In a conversation in July 2012, during the writing of these paragraphs, Micah Hanks, prominent futurist and author, said to me:

I think when one begins to look at the anthro-side of things, our inherent humanity is put in new perspective for us. It becomes easy to dismiss any kind of divinity at that point. But divinity is faith...in what? Faith cannot exist without the hope for something greater.... It is merely that glue which binds us to the divine. Whether or not a God exists, many have faith...and many who choose not to believe lack that faith, even if "he" is still there nonetheless. Or is our "faith" merely another human construct, much like thought, sight, and other things?

And, then, rather tongue-in-cheek, he added, "I would like to know if the Darsannee of Plibius TE-17 with their cold stony moon have an equivalent word to our English 'faith.'"

We'll cover this in more detail later, but suffice it to say that at this point in our study the Hebrew Bible starts to look more and more as if it is, simply, the Hebrew *version* of greater and much older worldly events. Could the Old Testament be nothing more than mere religious myth as opposed to the absolute on the spiritual truth of the universe, as Judeo-Christianity teaches? The more we investigate our religious origins, through the many myths, legends, and dogmatic theologies out there, the more we find that the similarities are staggering. Is there a "one true religion," where God is the benevolent ruler of all that exists, or are all these collective mythologies simply different versions of common events, with common threads running throughout them all? Was there some "proto-religion" from which all ancient religions drew their basic information, or did there exist some magnificent story from which all religions built their versions of origins?

And what of this pervasive presence of the serpent that emerges not only in the Sumerian and Hebrew religions, but in many prevalent religious mythologies the world over? What of this supposed mysterious race of Reptilian beings that seems to run through the undercurrent of humanity's mythos? Are these creatures the mere stuffs of man's creation? The devils in the dark of the conspiratorial minded? Or are they the diaphanous stuff of ether?

Archaeology and Myth
ar·chae·ol·o·gy (noun)
> The recovery and study of material objects, such as graves, buildings, tools, artworks, and human remains for the purpose

of investigating the structure and behavior of past cultures. Archaeologists rely on physical remains as clues to the emergence and development of human societies and civilizations. Anthropologists, by contrast, interact with living people to study their cultures. (*The American Heritage New Dictionary of Cultural Literacy*)

myth (noun)

A traditional or legendary story, usually concerning some being or hero or event, with or without a determinable basis of fact or a natural explanation, esp. one that is concerned with deities and demigods and explains some practice, rite, or phenomenon of nature.

Stories or matter of this kind: realm of myth.

Any invented story, idea, or concept: His account of the event is pure myth.

An imaginary or fictitious thing or person.

An unproved or false collective belief that is used to justify a social institution. (*Collins English Dictionary, Complete & Unabridged, 10th Edition*)

I was recently part of a live debate where an archaeological PhD made the emphatic statement that myth was merely "mankind's fantasies" and nothing more. Though it's true that a myth can at times be a mere story, removing itself far from the status of reliable historical resource that the increasingly scientifically minded discipline of archaeo-anthropological disciplines would utilize, myths are not always as rooted in the realms of fantasy as the esteemed halls of academia might consider them to be. Of necessity to a richer understanding of our past, an interdisciplinary dialogue efficacious to the future development of both mythological and archaeological disciplines should exist. Perhaps, somewhere along the way, you will come to find that the union of archaeology and mythology is far from being grounded in the realm of fairytale.

In context to the subject matter of this book, I am hailing back to the creation story as written in the Old Testament of the Bible. Although the story of creation as told in the book of Genesis is not the first of humanity's creation stories, it is one that tends to be most familiar in a broader sense and contains the roots of this discussion, so it is there that I will begin this search for fact, buried deep within the religious machinations and mythologies of faith. Also note that, though we may be able to identify facts within the linguistics and stories of the ancient texts, there is still no real way to quantify those facts as being hard evidence as to how things actually happened. But the multiplicity of creation accounts spread across a multiplicity of cultures and religions does give us a visible common thread that, when viewed from "outside the box" of any particular religion or culture, presents a picture comprised of commonalities that are pan-cultural.

Does this merely underscore the notion that humanity's civilizations, cultures, and religions have all evolved in equal fashion as one another? Or does it establish that there is a common thread woven throughout all cultures, beginning with a singular, common event lost in primordial antiquity? Each subsequent culture then ascribes its own version of events, character names, and twists on the original story, remanufacturing it to adapt to their own values and politics, not to mention the un-pierceable veils—the individual accounts of encounters and experiences that cannot be substantiated, but that are wholly important to any consideration of these spiritualistic, therefore hyper-speculative things.

Adam, Eve, and the Prince

The Book of Genesis tells us that Adam and Eve were the first couple. Whether you believe they were real people evolved from lower species, metaphoric stick figures, mythological characters, or actual, living human beings spiritually set against a deeply encoded message, the Hebrew religion tells us that they were created by God and given dominion over a garden paradise, and commanded to not eat of certain fruit growing on certain trees, lest they "die." Period.

46

Enter, stage left, the trickster character Nachash [נָ, חָשׁ], the serpent. Although never identified in the text as Lucifer, Satan, or the Devil (those names being attributed to him much later in the biblical scriptures), this character has become religiously synonymous with the devilish figure who led humanity away from God, thereby ushering in original sin and the resultant fall of mankind from a state of grace before a holy God, placing humanity in need of a spiritual savior-redeemer. This serpent character is also established from that point forward as the evil force, ever-present and working to thwart the work of a gracious and loving God in the affairs of humanity. Nachash is the Hebrew word that, when translated into English means, "serpent; trickster; crafty magician, bringer of knowledge; illuminator; bright shining one." According to Psalm 82, "God," appearing in the singular version of the word *Elohim*, refers to the *other* gods of heaven—the "Divine Council"—as the Elohim [אלהים], using the very same Hebrew word in its plural version, also calling them the "bright, shining Princes of Heaven." In this instance, you have the God of the Hebrew Bible declaring the existence of a "caste of gods" or "minor gods" over which He has authority, but whom he calls by the same name. Note that He never refers to them as "angels." The Hebrew word for angels (*mal'ahk* [מַ, לְאָךְ], which means "messenger") never appears in the passage.

Noted Hebrew and ancient Semitic language scholar Michael S. Heiser put it this way:

> ...[I]n light of the serpentine appearance of divine beings
> in Yahweh's presence, what we have in Genesis chapter three
> is wordplay.... *That is, Eve was not talking to a snake. She was
> speaking to an bright, shining upright being who was serpentine
> in appearance, and who was trying to bewitch her with lies.*
> (Heiser's emphasis)[9]

In other words, Eve was in the presence of one of the Sons of God. These beings were not angelic in nature, but were beings that possessed free will, and were more powerful than the angels, the messengers of God. When Psalm 8:4–5 speaks of the creation of human beings, utilizing the phrase "a little lower than the angels," the Hebrew text actually renders this as "a little lower than the Elohim." Eve was actually interacting with a member of the Divine Council who did not share God/Yahweh's enthusiasm for his new creation, human beings.

I am convinced, by ancient linguistic use of the same word, that the Serpent in the Garden of Eden story is one of these bright shining princes of heaven who is none other than the "bright shining one" who appears in the Genesis account of Adam and Eve as Nachash, the serpent character, who "seduces" and impregnates Eve, after she sits at his feet to learn the knowledge he bestows.

Believe what you will, as your faith might dictate regarding the connection to Lucifer, the Star of the Morning, the "Bright Shining Presence of the Glory of God," but the big question to ask is whether or not this teaching in the Hebrew scripture is a factual accounting or an elaborate cover story for much deeper events involving much more detail. We will, most probably, never know if Adam and Eve or Nachash ever existed, outside the realm of a faith story. But historical evidence does exist that links all these characters to other personages in different creation mythologies throughout many other ancient religious cultures, establishing a common thread or under-current, as we will see later in this chapter.

Let me say again, at this still-early point in this study, that it is not my intent to offend anyone's religious or spiritual beliefs or sensibilities. Nor is it my desire to trounce scientific research or input. My personal background is one that has its foundations in the Christian faith and academia; that is where I received all of my formal-yet-incomplete biblical training and seminary education, and I must state again, for emphasis, that I do not by any means wish to dissuade anyone from believing what they trust by faith in their own heart to be true. I would like to present some questions, however, throughout the entirety of this book that may challenge those beliefs. When making comparative forays into religious teachings that span many different cultures, one is left to decipher the messages and determine in his own heart that which he believes to be true and that which he must discard as false, not to mention what one can or cannot accept as fact on the basis of archaeological and anthropological research—two schools of study that must completely separate themselves from faith issues in order to retain integrity in fact-finding. (As with my previous work on the Nephilim, I am sure that there will be some who will fear for the eternal salvation of my soul, if not the backslidden state of my position with the Christian God.)

Suffice it to say that our personal faiths and religions—if adhered to—play harsh taskmasters in our lives and with what we understand to be our eternal souls. Add to that faith mix, the necessity of stepping back to examine other theologies outside its reach, then blend them all together with mythology, and you will find that there may exist something else completely different lying beneath the surface. There just may be things in the anthro-archaeo-mythological record that challenges you to look beyond the limits of your religious affiliations and think outside the box.

Slaves and Freedom Fighters

"[While] the Annunaki are sitting before you,

...Belet-ili the womb-goddess is present,

Let the womb-goddess create offspring,

And let man bear the load of the gods!

...Create primeval man that he may bear the yoke!

Let him bear the yoke, the work of Elil,

Let man bear the yoke of the gods!"

—Atrahasis, Tablet 1[10]

49

Cuneiform tablet containing the Atrahasis Epic, housed in the British Museum. Image made available through Wikimedia Commons.

Let's go back a little further than the writing of Genesis to the ancient Mesopotamian civilization of Sumer. According to their ancient cuneiforms, they were ruled by the Annuna/Annunaki, their god-caste of beings who came to the earth from the heavens. As the story goes, these gods, weary of performing their own manual labor, bred into—or genetically engineered and manipulated the DNA of—the humans of the Mesopotamian region who roamed as wild beasts. They did this to create a slave caste to do their work for them. As the story continues to unfold, the humans began to feel the weight of their enslavement. Theirs was an unwilling servitude. Accordingly, as time went on, the cruel hand of the slave masters became unbearable to the humans, and some of the Annunaki overlords went rogue, launching a conspiracy to free the humans and teach them the knowledge of science and spirituality, and the art of civilization, thus elevating them to the same god-like status as the Annunaki. The leader of the rebel freedom fighters was none other than Elil's brother god, an Annunaki named Enki, also known as Ea in the neighboring Akkadian culture.

When seeking to understand any ancient text, it is important to recognize a few things up-front:

1. The language in which it was written, as most ancient languages have a logic all their own that does not translate as well into modern English.

2. The people for whom the stories were being written. Their understanding of the stories and the way in which they were presented could have been vastly different than what we understand in a modern reading.

3. The context of the text in relation to the people for whom it was being written. Again, our current-day understanding being completely different as to what ancient peoples' would be.

The poetic, picturesque language of these ancient Sumerian texts, though beautiful in their presentation as ancient religious accounts, offer no source to quantify their veracity, thereby leaving themselves to stand only as religious history and myth. The importance of sources and verifiable information matter wholly when deciphering ancient texts, but five to seven thousand years ago, there was little need for this, if there existed even the slightest concept that far in the future, archaeologists, historians, and anthropologists would be far greater served had the ancients included indexes and bibliographies along with their cuneiform tablets. These accounts were written as religious history, in their context, and presented to the people of that time and place. The writers were establishing spiritual stories and a history of the origins of their people, but they were not presenting that information for the ages.

Zechariah Sitchin. Image made available through Wikimedia Commons.

In modern day, their stories have certainly been over-romanticized in the works of the late Zechariah Sitchin, who, while perhaps being "on to something," pushed his theories too far in order to make things fit. But despite his mistranslations and abused usages of ancient text, he did create an intriguing fictional account of the descent of extraterrestrial beings to the earth, housing the Sumerian mythology in updated, vernacular narrative. A prime example is when Sitchin forced the word *Nephilim* to mean "people of the firey rockets."[11] Sitchin, at best, simply mistranslated the word, ignoring—or misunderstanding—the Aramaic usage blended with biblical Hebrew. The Nephilim were not the ones who "came down" from anywhere. They were the descendents—the offspring—of those who actually did come down—namely, the Watchers, the "Sons of God," the bene ha 'Elohim [בְּנֵי־הָאֱלֹהִים] of Genesis chapter six. At worst, Sitchin deliberately ignored linguistics and fabricated meanings in order to substantiate his personal theories. But it is easy to understand how he may have extrapolated word definition from the combination of language and pictographs, as many of the carvings and reliefs from ancient Sumer depict their gods as descending in winged or bowl-like craft.

First-millennium seal showing descending Annunaki. Pictured is a worshipper and a fish-garbed sage before a stylized tree with a crescent moon and the descending winged disk set in the sky above it. Behind this group is another plant-form with a radiant star and the Star-Cluster (Pleiades cluster) above. In the background is the dragon of Marduk with Marduk's spear and Nabu's standard upon its back. Image made available through Wikimedia Commons.

The bigger issue is that Sitchin, in desiring to update the mythology and bring it into a more relevant understanding of ancient astronaut theory, simply did not do his homework. He, rather, like many of the theoretical metaphysicists of our age, stated that things were so, based solely on his (mis)interpretation of language, and his continual forcing of the square peg into the round hole. It's like grasping to the farthest possible meaning of a word—the broadest associative definition—and utilizing that obscure definition as the rock solid basis for your hypothesis. That can only end in disastrous interpretation and ultimately faulty conclusions.

When Sitchin refers to the Nephilim as the "people of the firey rockets," he has gone far out of his way and deep into a misunderstanding of the Sumerian language in order to establish his hypothesis. His argument for "ancient rockets" and "firey space flight" is constructed completely on two ancient Sumerian words, *mu* and *me*,[12] which are the same words as the Akkadian *shamu*, and the Hebrew *shem*. Continuing in his argument to establish the ancient space craft theory, Sitchin goes on to contend that the Tower of Babel account in Genesis, in which the people wanted to make for themselves a shem, is in reality describing the construction of a flying craft or rocket of some sort. In his book *The Twelfth Planet*, Sitchin defines the Sumerian word *mu* as meaning "an oval shaped, conical object," as well as "that which rises straight."[13]

The problem is that Mr. Sitchin merely defines the word, but offers up no linguistic etymology to define it within the framework of Sumerian language. He simply states the meaning and continues on building his hypothesis. However, it is interesting to note that the ancient Sumerians created their own dictionary,[14] and it contains the word *mu*! The entry in the ancient Sumerian dictionary has the word *mu* being symonymous with the Akkadian word *shamu*, meaning "heaven, part of the sky, (sometimes) rain." This is what the word means according to ancient scribes, who make no mention of flying craft or fiery rocket ships. It is a simple descriptive noun for the sky. The Sumerian word *me* is used for the same meaning, as part of the heavens.

And that's just the linguistics. Zechariah Sitchin represents, to me, a man who had a deep-set interest in discovering who we are and where we came from. His research into ancient Mesopotamian culture to look for ancient answers is admirable, while all at once woefully incomplete and academically insincere.

Peter James, coauthor of the controversial book *Centuries of Darkness*, has leveled his own criticisms against Sitchin's scholarship, pointing out that he not only deliberately had to disregard the rest of the known world outside Sumer and Mesopotamian civilization, but also for his seemingly innate misunderstanding of Babylonian literature:

> [Sitchin] uses the Epic of Creation Enuma Elish as the foundation for his cosmogony, identifying the young god Marduk, who overthrows the older regime of gods and creates the Earth, as the unknown "Twelfth Planet." In order to do so, he interprets the Babylonian theogony as a factual account of the birth of the other "eleven" planets. The Babylonian names for the planets are established beyond a shadow of a doubt— Ishtar was the deity of Venus, Nergal of Mars, and Marduk of Jupiter—and confirmed by hundreds of astronomical/ astrological tables and treatises on clay tablets and papyri from the Hellenistic period. Sitchin merrily ignores all this and assigns unwarranted planetary identities to the gods mentioned in the theogony. For example, Apsu, attested as god of the primeval waters, becomes, of all things, the Sun! Ea, as it suits Sitchin, is sometimes planet Neptune and sometimes a spaceman. And the identity of Ishtar as the planet Venus, a central feature of Mesopotamian religion, is nowhere mentioned in the book—instead Sitchin arbitrarily assigns to Venus another deity from *Enuma Elish,* and reserves Ishtar for a role as a female astronaut.[15]

William Irwin Thompson, well-known social philosopher and cultural critic (ergo: a man who make his living criticizing and poking tongue-in-cheek jabs), writer and publisher of poetry throughout his career, and a recipient of the Oslo International Poetry Festival Award in 1986, describes his personal writing and speaking style as mind-jazz on ancient texts. Thompson had this to say about what he calls Sitchin's "literalism":

> What Sitchin sees is what he needs for his hypothesis. So figure 15 on page 40 is radiation therapy, and figure 71 on

page 136 is a god inside a rocket-shaped chamber. If these are gods, why are they stuck with our cheap B movie technology of rockets, microphones, space-suits, and radiation therapy? If they are gods, then why can't they have some really divine technology such as intradimensional worm-hole travel, antigravity, starlight propulsion, or black hole bounce rematerializations? Sitchin has constructed what appears to be a convincing argument, but when he gets close to single images on ancient tablets, he falls back into the literalism of "Here is an image of the gods in rockets." Suddenly, ancient Sumer is made to look like the movie set for *Destination Moon*. Erich Von Däniken's potboiler *Chariots of the Gods?* has the same problem. The plain of Nazca in Peru is turned into a World War II landing strip. The gods can cross galactic distances, but by the time they get to Peru, their spaceships are imagined as World War II prop jobs that need an enormous landing strip. This literalization of the imagination doesn't make any sense, but every time it doesn't, you hear Sitchin say "There can be no doubt, but..."[16]

This is what disturbs me most about Zechariah Sitchin.

As someone who is invested in wanting to know more about our origins, and who is thoroughly intrigued with the ancient astronaut theory, I have to admit that such small words as *mu* and *me* can redefine the entire theory as put forward by Sitchin, who I still contend has some good ideas brewing, but has relied too heavily—and foolheartedly—on his own translations and, perhaps even deliberate, squeezing of a definition to fit his overall theory.

Folks, language is important. It is so important that even the Bible refers to itself as a book that is so "God-breathed," that it is "infallible" and cannot be changed by "one jot or tittle" (Matthew 5L18)—the tiniest of Hebrew punctuation marks. Simply put, the writers of Hebrew scripture were *using language as a gage of authenticity.* That is an ultimately strong point on which theories can rise or fall, and we have archaeologists to thank for the deciphering of ancient mythological texts. Who knew a five-thousand-year-old dictionary would come in so handy? I wish Sitchin had referred to it, as that would, for me, not cast such broad dispersions on his interpretations and subsequent theories.

Does this—or should it—delegitimize Sitchin's theories and his dozen-plus books on the topic? A most definitive *yes* on my part. If you are going to present theory based on scholarship, would it not be important to first ensure that the scholarship is sound?

In turn, should this, then, delegitimize ancient alien theory that adheres to similar yet differing hypothesis as Sitchin's? Not necessarily. Better scholarship on the topic needs to be established. And in the end, we may not come up drawing the same conclusions that were the object of our original hypothesis.

In Sumerian mythology, Enki ("Ea" in the neighboring Akkadian religion) is the god of craft, mischief, intelligence, and knowledge. He is also known as the god over the waters and creation, and although

Enki from a ninth-century BCE Babylonian alabaster wall-panel relief. Copyright Trustees of the British Museum. Image used by permission of the British Museum.

57

the exact meaning of his name is uncertain, the common translation is "Lord of the Earth." When you compare him to Nachash in the Book of Genesis, you find similar definitions as the "trickster" and bringer of "mischief." When you keep in mind the etymology of "making mischief," you will find that its origins have little to do with what we consider to be mischief by modern standards. Mischief was in its earliest forms equated with chaos, havoc, and the committing of rebellious acts.

There is such overt similarity between the acts of Enki/Ea and the serpent in the Garden of Eden in the Book of Genesis that it cannot be overlooked. The traditional story tells us that the serpent is none other than Satan, the Devil, Lucifer. However, the serpent is never called by any of those names in the text. Those are names attributed to the serpent thousands of years later in other scriptural writings of the Hebrew Bible. What is clear is that Nachash, the serpent character in the Eden story, is a member of the Divine Council, the Elohim. As I covered extensively in *The Rise and Fall of the Nephilim,* Psalm 82 presents a caste of minor gods referred to as the Elohim, the "bright, shining Princes of Heaven."[17] This plural form of the word *Elohim* was uttered in the text by the singular Elohim, who equates them to himself.

For most evangelicals, there is a problem in that the Old Testament, here, affirms the existence of a multiplicity of Elohim. Though simple, the solution requires us to think like an ancient Semitic Israelite, and not as a product of the Reformation or the modern evangelicalism that exists today. Biblical theology did not begin with modern evangelicalism, the Calvins, the Luthers, the Aquinases, or even the Augustines. It began with the ancient text as it stands, understood within the historical, cultural, and religious context that produced it.

The first occurrence of *Elohim* [אלהים] is correctly translated "God" and is obviously to be taken as the singular form of the word for reasons of grammatical subject-verb agreement. The second use of the word

Elohim in this passage is to be equally understood as being in the plural form because it is the object of the sentence's preposition. The grammar and syntax are crystal clear in this psalm, in that a singularity cannot preside from within a singularity. It is clear by the language of the text that Elohim (the singular) is presiding over the Elohim (the plural), and it is repeated a second time later in the short psalm. Both "God" and the "gods" are represented by the identical word *Elohim* [אלהים].[18]

It Must Be Satan!

By definition, Nachash, the bright shining one (later, he becomes known as Lucifer, who in his pre-fallen state is the bright shining presence and defender of the glory of God, "The Bright and Morning Star"—which is also a reference to the Messiah/Jesus, much later; more on this in the next chapter), is also known as "the bringer of knowledge and intelligence, the illuminator." When Nachash seduced Eve by the offering of "forbidden fruit"—that forbidden information that would make humans "just as Elohim (gods)" (Genesis 3:22)—he became the bringer of knowledge and the emancipator of the intellect, for after the forbidden fruit was accepted and eaten, the humans knew that they were naked. They knew that there was more to their existence than simply caring for the garden for the superior being who bred them.

> And the LORD God said, "The man has now become like one
> of us, knowing good and evil. He must not be allowed to reach
> out his hand and take also from the tree of life and eat, and live
> forever." 23So the LORD God banished him from the Garden
> of Eden to work the ground from which he had been taken.
> Genesis 3:22–23

The Sumerian tablets tell us that the rebel god named Enki/Ea was the extraterrestrial (not-of-this-earth, non-human) being appointed by the chief god of the Annunaki, Elil, to create Homo sapiens. After his involvement with the original genetic experiment that bequeathed the slave race of humans, bred to do the work for the Annunaki (as paralleled in the keepers of the Garden of Eden in the Book of Genesis) his compassion for the plight of the slave race shifted his role as a genetic engineer to that of a veritable "rebel leader." His actions flew in the face of the rest of his kind.

> Now there was one Atrahasis
> Whose ear was open (to) his god Enki.
> He would speak wih his god
> And his god would speak with him.
> Atrahasis made his voice heard
> And spoke to his lord,
> "How long [will the gods make us suffer]?
> Will they make us suffer illness forever?"
> Enki made his voice heard
> And spoke to his servent:
> "Call the elders, the senior men!
> Start [an uprising] in your own house,
> Let heralds proclaim…
> Let them make a loud noise in the land:
> Do not revere your gods,
> Do not pray to your goddesses…"
>
> —from: Atrahasis 1:vii[19]

It is also related in the Sumerian texts that Ea's headquarters of operation were in the swampy, backwater region called the Snake Marsh, also referred to as a *den* to many reptiles and serpents. In other words, the first fight for freedom of the human race took place in an area known as "Ea-Den."

Enki/Ea was originally the god of the ancient Sumerian city, Eridu, known for being the first and oldest city mentioned throughout Sumerian literature. It is closely associated with Uruk ("First City") as built in biblical tradition by Cain, the Nephilim son of Eve and Nachash.[20]

Closely associated with the city of Eridu is the mythical region below the earth's surface, known as the Abzu,[21] which is often interpreted as an underground sweet water ocean in Mesopotamian mythology.[22]

The ancient city of Eridu as envisioned by archaeological artist Balage Balogh. Used by permission from the artist, www.archaeologyillustrated.com.

The geographical characteristics and features of the ancient site of the city of Eridu must have had great impact both physically and spiritually with the original concept of the Abzu. It is difficult to imagine what exactly made the place sacred to the ancient Sumerians, mostly due to the fact that there are no direct references or depictions of the original landscape and terrain. However, where there was water in these arid, desert regions, there was life, and it was in these geographical places that civilizations were established and flourished. Eridu was situated in a marshy and continuously flooded area in the backwaters of the Tigris and Euphrates rivers, where it can be easily deduced by geographical patterns that some natural phenomenon of flooding and receding marsh waters took place, and was perceived by the ancient inhabitants of Eridu to be sacred nature at work.

The concept of the Abzu was derived from the waterways and clear lagoons that encompassed the city of Eridu. The surrounding river backwaters were also referred to as a "marshy den" that physically created a sanctuary setting, enclosing the sacred city, where eventually, a cult arose, dedicated to the god and/or goddess of sweet water.[23]

The earliest form of the god Enki could have been "Abzu," who was later seen as being conquered or vanquished by Enki,[24] who then stepped into the place of Abzu, which in turn became known as his domain.[25] This sort of alteration of concepts, where an ancient deity becomes a mere attribute of a more contemporary, evolved, divine figure, was a common attributable alteration when the god took on the function or act of a certain deed or natural phenomena, such as took place in the rising and falling of the waters surrounding Eridu. And make no mistake, the changing of the names of deities was common practice among the ancients, this being clearly illustrated in the many names for God in the Old Testament (Jehovah, Elohim, El Shaddai, Adoni, the Angel of Lord, and many others) as well as the biblical record of the divine changing of names of some of the early patriarchs—Abram of Ur becoming Abraham, Jacob becoming Israel, Joseph being renamed by the Egyptians as Zaphnath-paaneah, Saul of Tarsus renamed Paul the Apostle, and even the Messiah had evolutionary progressive name changes and additions as the function of the Messiah grew and burgeoned: Kinsman Redeemer, the Lion of Judah, the Lamb of God, the Rod of Jesse (of the royal house of King David, which did not exist until thousands of years after the earliest form of Messiah was used), and so on. The meanings of names was all-important in ancient religion, and the owner of the name change generally followed the rule of *change equates function, designation, or purpose.*

In antiquity, one deity might have had several names used for him simultaneously, as mentioned previously with the several names for God and Messiah in the Hebrew Bible. During the course of time as older names disappeared or developed into newer forms with greater contemporary meaning, the older name incorporated as an attribute of his newer function. However, it should be taken into consideration that an original meaning of the name of a deity might mean nothing at all to a community of people using that name many centuries after the name was first uttered.

Look to the Tetragrammaton, the paleo-Hebrew name of the god YHWH (Jehovah). It must have had a translatable meaning, very early on, prior to the writing of the Hebrew scriptures, when the Hebrew religion was in an early state of development, and still in its infancy. Yet, much later, when Moses composed the Hebrew Scriptures around 1400 BCE, which also contained the Law for the Hebrew people, establishing the foundations of the Jewish religion, demonstrates signs that the name YHWH was still rather ambiguous and had no direct translation. And it is highly possible that the original meaning of YHWH had no importance whatsoever for the Hebrews who lived much later, where in the fifth century BCE they used several divine names for God, all more than likely referring to older deities in older layers of Israelite religion. The form and pronunciation of YHWH, although considered as sacred, as was the deity behind the name itself, was never altered. It was simply retained as part of the growing list of attributable names for the Hebrew God.

All of this is highly important to understanding the name of Enki/Ea, the evolution of his name being much similar. Even if Enki/Ea once had a clearly translatable meaning that was understandable to ancient Sumerian people, that original meaning was not necessarily understood by the Mesopotamian people living in the third millennium city-states of Sumer and neighboring Akkad. But the name Enki—specifically the Akkadian version, Ea—did migrate into the Canaanite region from the Mesopotamian region throughout the course of the following millennia and a half. The name *Ea* became the base of the Canaanite word *YHWH* (pronounced "Yee-ah-weh"), the Hebrew name *Jehovah*. This is all important in understanding how the idea of the serpent became the basis for the Genesis account of the Garden of Eden's Serpent character, Nachash.

The direct translation of the Sumerian name, Enki, recorded as a divine Sumerian name in written sources since the composition of the texts literally translated as "Lord Earth," or "Lord of the Earth," extending to the meaning of "he who ruled beneath the earth (the Abzu) and had dominion over it."[26]

Sounds like Satan, doesn't it? The problem is that, although Enki/ Ea has incredible mythological linkage to the Serpent in the Bible, the name Ea is the early form of the name *YHWH*—Jehovah. There is some sort of twist in meaning that has taken place along the millennia, and there is some theoretical, yet highly heretical, surmising that the two characters are, perhaps, one in the same: Lucifer and Jehovah, at least etymologically, if not theologically. Were they both of the pantheon of the Elohim? The connectivity between Enki/Ea, who brought forbidden knowledges of the gods to early humans from a place known as the Snake Den (Ea's Den), is undeniably connected to the character of Nachash, who was the illuminator and bringer of forbidden knowledge to Adam and Eve in the Genesis story of the Garden of Eden, yet he is etymologically linked to Jehovah, the savior of humanity.

Chapter Two

That's Not What I Learned in Sunday School

If you grew up anything like me, you attended Sunday school as a kid. Maybe you even attended as an adult, and perhaps you still attend today. I only talk about religious education in the framework of "Sunday school," as it gives a quick reference in our minds to all the things we were taught in our religious training as kids. It's there that we learned in rudimentary form all the basic stories of the Bible and the embryonic systematic theology that formed our particular denomination's dogmas and doctrines. If you were Catholic, you went to Catechism. If Lutheran, you attended Confirmation classes. If Jewish, you attended synagogue and both pre- and post- bar and bat mitzvah education, and maybe even went on into Medrichim in your teens. Perhaps you are of a different faith altogether or experienced no form of biblical training at all. Most of us have some notion as to what the early stories of the bible had to say regarding the creation of mankind, the Garden of Eden, Noah and the Ark, and other great stories that are religious in their origins, but that have transcended into common dialogue through the countless retellings and spread into pop culture, children's books, toys, games, and all sorts of other ancillary forms throughout the years.

For the purposes of this examination, as I have stated, I hail back to the roots of my Christian education, as they are the foremost familiar tales stemming from much older, not-so-familiar historical religious accounts and mythologies. If I were to approach an absolute stranger on the street and ask him or her about the Garden of Eden or the Serpent in the Garden or Noah's Ark, a great flood, or even Moses and the Ten Commandments, he or she would, as would most people, have some idea of what it is I was asking. These are common stories woven into the fabric of our religious heritage; that is not to say *your* particular heritage, but the heritage and religious "mythology" of humanity. In many cases, the old adage rings true that familiarity breeds contempt, and many of us, though perhaps adhering to what we were taught as children, have drifted far from those original teachings, relegating them to the realm of fantasy and religious fairytale.

As I grew older, I began to question many of the things I had been taught. I knew that I accepted those old stories as the absolute truth of God's Word as I was taught to do as a youngster, and they became engrained in my mind as some sort of probable universal truth. But because I extended my biblical education into my teens and young adult years, I found that my logical mind contended with the faith stories that made so much sense so many years earlier. I questioned who God really was, what His names meant, and why there were so many things in the pages of scripture that seemed to play like a *Lord of the Rings* movie, only with angels on crack.

So, I started asking questions.

"Why does the name Elohim have a plural connotation?"

"What!? Beings came down from heaven and impregnated humans?! Who were they?"

"Why did Moses never name the pharaohs with whom he had his encounters? Isn't that important to the narrative?"

"Was Goliath actually a real giant?"

"What the hell are 'sea monsters' and 'leviathan'?"

"What is that wheel-within-a-wheel-within-a-wheel
   contraption in Ezekiel?"

"Why is it Leviticus placed a legal mandate against eating
   Alaskan King Crab?"

"What? I can't have sex with a menstruating woman?"

And so on, and so on, and so on.

Those were only the tip of the iceberg when it came to my questions. Many more dealt with textual criticisms, historical references, the mention of constellations that played important roles in pagan religions but figured prominently in biblical passages, homosexuality, Old Testament patriarchal polygamy, the genocide of infidels, the drinking of alcoholic beverages, and the mandate for women to stay silent in the church while allowing them to teach classes and sing.

The questions listed here are not just examples I've pulled out of the air, but all actual questions I asked, among many others, while attending Bible school and seminary, and working in youth ministry in my teens and 20s. Ultimately, I was labeled a troublemaker. This moniker was delivered in one of two forms: "You are a troublemaker, Mr. Roberts. That kind of thinking will get you nowhere, fast, around here," and "You are a troublemaker, Mr. Roberts"—wink-wink-nudge-nudge, accompanied by the non-verbal "And you are on to something by asking, but we can't talk about that here, in this setting," which ended up in private, out-of-the-way chats over cups of coffee in dark corners of far-away cafés.

As in most theological, dogma-driven circles, questioning the norm generally lands you in hot water. But the biggest question of them all, for me, was this: "Why? How do we know that what we believe and teach is the absolute corner on the truth? Did God descend and tell us these things firsthand, or are we simply believing in something for which we have no proof and for which all the science and reason and logic out there seems to contradict? Is that the true nature of faith?" I'd ask, bewildered, "Believing something that makes no sense for a greater purpose of which we have absolutely no proof?"

"It's better than believing in nothing at all," I was admonished with some conclusive air.

That is what has brought me to the place where I write about these things. I do not disbelieve in God, nor have I thrown out the baby with the bathwater, but I do have questions for which answers are hard to come by within the context of my religion. So I started looking outside the box, to the places that might lend me some better perspective or some answers that might give more solidity to the foundation that I was told was as "solid as the Rock of Christ. Amen and Glory!"

The Serpent in the Garden

[1]Now the snake was the most clever of all the wild animals the Lord God had made. One day the snake said to the woman, "Did God really say that you must not eat fruit from any tree in the garden?" [2]The woman answered the snake, "We may eat fruit from the trees in the garden. [3]But God told us, "You must not eat fruit from the tree that is in the middle of the garden. You must not even touch it, or you will die."" [4]But the snake said to the woman, "You will not die. [5]God knows that if you eat the fruit from that tree, you will learn about good and evil and you will be like God!" [6]The woman saw that the tree was beautiful, that its fruit was good to eat, and that it would make her wise. So she took some of its fruit and ate it. She also gave some of the fruit to her husband who was with her, and he ate it. [7]Then, it was as if their eyes were opened. They realized they were naked, so they sewed fig leaves together and made something to cover themselves. [8]Then they heard the Lord God walking in the garden during the cool part of the day, and the man and his wife hid from the Lord God among the trees in the garden. [9]But the Lord God called to the man and said, "Where are you?" [10]The man answered, "I heard you walking in the garden, and I was afraid because I was naked, so I hid."

11God asked, "Who told you that you were naked? Did you eat fruit from the tree from which I commanded you not to eat?" 12The man said, "You gave this woman to me and she gave me fruit from the tree, so I ate it." 13Then the Lord God said to the woman, "How could you have done such a thing?" She answered, "The snake tricked me, so I ate the fruit." 14The Lord God said to the snake, "Because you did this, a curse will be put on you. You will be cursed as no other animal, tame or wild, will ever be. You will crawl on your stomach, and you will eat dust all the days of your life. 15I will make you and the woman enemies to each other. Your descendants and her descendants will be enemies. One of her descendants will crush your head, and you will bite his heel." 16Then God said to the woman, "I will cause you to have much trouble when you are pregnant, and when you give birth to children, you will have great pain. You will greatly desire your husband, but he will rule over you."

17Then God said to the man, "You listened to what your wife said, and you ate fruit from the tree from which I commanded you not to eat. So I will put a curse on the ground, and you will have to work very hard for your food. In pain you will eat its food all the days of your life. 18The ground will produce thorns and weeds for you, and you will eat the plants of the field. 19You will sweat and work hard for your food. Later you will return to the ground, because you were taken from it. You are dust, and when you die, you will return to the dust." 20The man named his wife Eve, because she was the mother of all the living. 21The Lord God made clothes from animal skins for the man and his wife and dressed them. 22Then the Lord God said, "Humans have become like one of us; they know good and evil. We must keep them from eating some of the fruit from the tree of life, or they will live forever." 23So the Lord God forced Adam out of the garden of Eden to work the ground from which he was taken. 24After God forced humans out of the garden, he placed angels and a sword of fire that flashed around in every direction on its eastern border. This kept people from getting to the tree of life. (Genesis 3:1–24)

Taking a biblical story and dissecting it to bare all the internal organs and skeletal structure is a meticulously important process necessary in an understanding of ancient culture. Simply said, the Bible, for all of its gloriously revered tales of Jehovah God and His interactions with His human creation, spawning three of the world's major religions, is a source point for understanding the ancient anthropology of humanity. Depending on your view of the veracity of biblical scripture, there is no shadow of doubt that its pages reveal stories, accounts, myths, legends, and fables that mirror—or are mirrored by—a plethora of cultures in the ancient world. The importance of the Bible, if not for faith and practice, is to see it as a book that demonstrates another facet of events as experienced and recounted by ancient mankind—a *version,* if you will, of common events experienced by ancient humanity.

Accordingly, if you are of Judeo-Christian or Muslim religious heritage, the pages of these religious texts and biblical scripture are Truth. According to certain Christian denominations (and a phrase I heard over and over throughout my Bible education!), "The Bible is the only foundation and authority for faith and practice." Although this may or may not be true, it is clear that when one takes a step back from the text of the Bible, removing the sometimes-rose-colored glasses of dogma and systematic theology, you can start to read between the lines and see, as it were, the vastness of the world flickering between the slats as you walk along the perimeter fence of one of the world's most holiest of books.

And there exist many other world cultures that have varying accounts of creation and the first family, some of which border on that fairytale sort of scenario, such as gods or great human warriors casting beasts and animals into the skies to create the swath of heavenly constellations. African and Native American accounts of creation share such commonalities such as subterranean humans coming to the surface of the earth and "gods" from the heavens impregnating their beautiful daughters with quadruplets.

For example, in Lakota, accounts of the first human family, Waziya, the Old Man, and his wife, Wakanka, emerged for the first time out into the world from underground. Wakanka gave birth to Ite, a daughter so beautiful that she captivated the attentions of Tate, the God of the Wind, who married her and fathered quadruplets. In this account, we are told of a character, Iktomi the Trickster, who tempted that first family with promises of great wealth, power, and beauty. Iktomi bears great resemblance to the Old Testament's account of the serpent, Nachash, who tempted Eve in the Garden of Eden, promising eternal life and knowledge like that of the gods if she ate of the forbidden tree at the garden's center. As with the Lakota tale of Waziya, Wakanka, and Ite, disobedience and treachery against God/the gods resulted in banishment from paradise for them all. Nachash and his Lakota counterpart, Iktomi, were cursed and exiled to the earth for all time, while the first families went on to bear children and spread throughout the world.

It is very interesting to note that although Waziya and Wakanka "came out from underground," according to Lakota oral tradition, in the Genesis account (2:7), Adam was "formed out of the clay of the ground." The similarities in cultural versions of creation can be clearly seen. All the varied cultural tales of creation have such a vast number of similarities and overlaps that the touch points create a tangled web of scientific methodology, established more by the crossovers in the myths of various cultures, rather than the veracity of the individual cultural tale.

In the Hebrew account of creation's first family, in the Genesis text, Adam and Eve were the first human couple, created by God and placed in a beautiful paradise garden called Eden. Their mandate was to till the ground and keep it (the garden) for God, the only prohibition being the eating of fruit from the two forbidden trees, the Tree of the Knowledge of Good and Evil and the Tree of Life, located at the center of the garden. Along comes the Serpent, out of nowhere, with no contextual link to the passage, and tempts Eve to eat of the fruit of one of the forbidden trees.

Eve looks at the fruit, and finds it beautiful and tasty in appearance, as well as something that would make her wise. How she knows that the fruit will bring her wisdom is absent from the narrative. She plucks the fruit, eats it, and offers it to her husband, Adam, who according to the text, just happened to be standing there with her, saying nothing nor offering any protest to her actions or the temptations of the Serpent. The result is an instantaneous opening of the floodgates of their minds, and they are suddenly fully aware that they are naked. They run and hide, covering themselves with fig leaves they've sewn together, while the Serpent seems to fall silent. The consequences are devastating to the human race, in that God finds the couple, curses them for disobeying his decrees, and condemns forever all of humanity. He also curses the Serpent, condemning him to crawl forever on his belly and be reviled above all other animals on the earth, and that his offspring and the offspring of the mother of humanity would forever be in enmity and conflict.

That's about as mythological a tale as they come, rife with all the earmarks of every other culture's mythological tales. But in Judeo-Christianity, we are taught that this is the truth, breathed from God, Himself. So, either one of two things is true:

1. It's a myth, not unlike the creation myths of many other cultures, or

2. Mythological tales are sometimes the absolute truth, despite resembling the mythological tales of all other cultures.

Perhaps you could add a third option:

3. It's the truth, and all other mythological tales sourced in other cultures are simply those other culture's twist on the truth, and are the work of Satan performing acts of diabolical mimicry.

There is more to the Eden tale than what you read on the surface. And whether you believe the account to be fact, fiction, allegory, or myth, there is an encoded message deep within the subtext of the passage. The story of the Garden of Eden's occupants and their fall from grace is more than a simple tale of disobedience and the eating of forbidden fruit. It is a tale of race interrupted—and it mirrors many of the events we find in the ancient Sumerian account of the Annunaki breeding and enslavement of primeval mankind.

In Eden, Eve's downfall came as a result of her encounter with the Serpent. The encoded message in the Genesis passage implies that she had intercourse with the Serpent character, thus rendering her recorded bite out of a piece of fruit, small potatoes.

The Serpent not only seduced Eve away from the arms of her husband Adam, but impregnated her and she conceived her son Cain. Eve, in turn, brought this sexual knowledge to her husband, Adam, and they also had sex, conceiving Abel, Cain's twin brother. But Nachash did much more. Buried in the encoded mythical tale, he also passed to the first couple the forbidden knowledge of the Elohim, the pantheon of gods ruled by Jehovah.

Comparatively, similar events took place when Enki/Ea went to the humans and incited rebellion against the gods by passing on their forbidden knowledge to the humans from his place in the Sanke Marsh, Ea's Den. The ancient Sumerian cuneiforms also tell that this was done against the wishes of his superior and brother god, Elil, and as punishment for this treasonous act, the progressive Enki/Ea and his followers were condemned and ordered to remain underground—in the earth, Abzu as their domain, within its vast cavernous systems weaving and intersecting throughout the substrata of the earth. Along with this punishment, it was ruled that Enki/Ea was to never interfere with humans again and that their generations would not only not ever know each other, but will learn to hate each other and be in continual conflict, just as God pronounced the "continual enmity" that would exist between the offspring of the Serpent and the offspring of the humans, in Genesis 3:14–15.

> In a rather tragic way for Western religious thought, then, the story seems to suggest that God stands against our own moral maturity, against sexuality, and against the divinization of human nature through the acquisition of knowledge and sexual pleasure. It also insinuates, when it does not actually shout, that we all die because our first parents knew each other within the intimate gnosis of sexual intercourse. Because they fucked, we're screwed.
> —Jeffrey J. Kripal, *The Serpent's Gift, Gnostic Reflections on the Study of Religion*

Have you ever encountered a serpent that walked upright? Spoke in an audible, understandable voice? According to Genesis, the snake that Eve encountered did both of these things. Though it is probably safe to say that Eve was not very experienced in the ways of the world, seeing as she was the very first woman, it is also probably very safe to say that she knew the difference between a snake and a man. According to the scripture (Genesis 3:1), this snake was neither:

> Now the serpent was more crafty than any of the wild animals the LORD God had made. He said to the woman, "Did God really say, 'You must not eat from any tree in the garden?'"

As mentioned, the Hebrew word used in the Book of Genesis for the word *serpent* is nachash (pronounced: naw-kawsh), meaning "magician or enchanter; a spellbinder; to illuminate, shine." Jewish Rabbinic interpretation never saw this word as meaning a literal snake. It was to be understood as "a shining being with power to enchant." This is a far cry from a snake in the grass, and in many later interpretations is identified as none other than Lucifer himself, although the passage never actually calls him by that name. It is attributed thousands of years later. It is this being that influences and beguiled Eve—or "seduced," in a more accurate sense—into eating the fruit of the forbidden tree in the midst of the Garden of Eden—which, as we have seen, had absolutely nothing to do with eating fruit from a tree.

> ²"The woman said to the serpent, "We may eat fruit from the trees in the garden, ³but God did say, 'You must not eat fruit from the tree that is in the middle of the garden, and you must not touch it, or you will die.'"
> (Genesis 3:2–3)

The following linguistic details of what transacted in the Genesis account of the Garden of Eden were presented in *The Rise and Fall of the Nephilim*, but well worth reconsidering here:

> The Hebrew word for that tree is *ets* [עֵץ], a word that is in very close association with the Hebrew word toledah [תּוֹלְדוֹת] both meaning "generations." It is from these words that we draw the modern equivalent of "family tree." Other variations of the word *ets* is "the wood of a tree as an opening and closing of a door." In an applicational stretch the same word can apply to the term "portal; opening of one's mind; enlightenment."[1]

It is highly suggested that the Tree of the Knowledge of Good and Evil, from which Eve is said to have eaten the forbidden fruit, was not a literal tree at all, but rather, symbolic of the pre-Adamic races that lived in the regions surrounding the Garden of Eden. These races are said to encompass the Atlantean civilization.

The phrase *fruit of the tree* is the Hebrew word *periy* [בְּרִי]—fruit: produce of the ground; offspring, children, progeny (of the womb); or figuratively: fruit (of actions). The phrase *eat of it* is the Hebrew word *'akal* [אָכַל]; this word has many uses, among which, one use means to lay with a woman (sexual intercourse); and the word *touch* is the Hebrew word *naga* [נגע]—to touch (that is, to lay the hand upon [for any purpose]; euphemism for: to touch, in a sexual manner).

> ⁴"You will not certainly die," the serpent said to the woman. ⁵"For God knows that when you eat of it your eyes will be opened, and you will be like God, knowing good and evil." ⁶When the woman saw that the fruit of the tree was good for food and pleasing to the eye, and also desirable for gaining wisdom, she took some and ate it. She also gave some to her husband, who was with her, and he ate it. ⁷Then the eyes of both of them were opened, and they realized they were naked; so they sewed fig leaves together and made coverings for themselves.
> (Genesis 3:4–7)

This was obviously no ordinary tree; in fact it wasn't a literal tree at all. Many biblical scholars interpret this as Lucifer. The definitions of some of the Hebrew words used here are controversial as to their application in this context. That is to say that there may be opinions that have already been drawn prior to extrapolating meanings and applying them to the context. Here are the words from this Hebrew passage: The phrase *pleasant to the eyes* is the Hebrew word *chamad* [מחמד]—to desire, to covet, to take pleasure in, to delight in, to be desirable, to delight greatly, to desire greatly, desirableness, preciousness. The word *desired* is the Hebrew word *ta'avah* [הואת] —to yearn for; to lust after (used of bodily appetites) a longing; by implication: a delight (subjectively, satisfaction, objectively, a charm): a desire, a wish, longings of one's heart; lust, an appetite, covetousness (in a bad sense); to covet; to wait longingly. *Took* is the Hebrew word *laqach* [לקח]—a primitive root; to take (in the widest variety of applications): to take, to lay hold of, to receive, to marry, to take a wife, to take to or for a person, to procure, to get, to take possession of, to select, to choose, to take in marriage, to receive, to accept.

Under these definitions, a very different picture of the Eve's temptation in the Garden of Eden emerges. The parsed passage shown is far more than a sinful, disobedient appreciation of fruit. All the references we hear of Eve eating an apple, or depictions in religious art of the Eden couple eating a big piece of fruit, are merely coded information and a hiding of what the passage truly speaks about. What really happened in this scene in the Garden of Eden is that Eve, the mother of humanity, lost her virginity to the Serpent, as you can see that she encountered him sexually before ever having sex with her husband, Adam. And further down the passage, the text is implicit that Eve was impregnated by this encounter. She then drew her husband into the scenario, and he willingly partook. And Eve also became impregnated by Adam. Eve was now bearing fraternal twins, Cain and Abel—one from the seed of Adam, and the other from the seed of the character who is known as the Serpent in the Garden.

The grand sin that was committed in Eden was not mere disobedience in the eating of a forbidden piece of fruit from a forbidden tree in the midst of the garden. It was a sexual sin that created a dual bloodline in the twins conceived in Eve's womb. According to the subsequent passages in Genesis, we learn that Abel was the blood seed of Adam, but that Cain was the blood seed of the Serpent and that the lineage would be in constant conflict with one another, starting with Cain murdering his twin brother.

This begins the trail of the Nephilim—the bloodlines of the serpent.

Blood Is Thicker Than Water

The Genesis record of the Serpent's sexual encounter with Eve, the "mother of all living," establishes that the biblical account recognizes a dual bloodline had been conceived in Eve. This fact is borne out, not only in the condemnations in Eden, post-fall, and the pronunciation of what is understood in rabbinic and evangelical schools to be the first Messianic prophecy (*"…and he will crush your head, but you will bite his heel"* [Genesis 3:15]) but also by the long lists of genealogies that appear in the subsequent Old Testament books. And these genealogies were written down and placed there for one purpose alone: to establish a traceable, pure human bloodline from which the Messiah would come. "Traceable to whom?" you might ask. Traceable back to the loins of Adam, the first human male. Here is how the genealogies began in the first 28 verses of 1 Chronicles, chapter 1:

Historical Records From Adam to Abraham to Noah's Sons

[1]Adam, [Author's Note: Take note of the exclusion of the firstborn twin sons, Cain and Abel] Seth, Enosh, [2]Kenan, Mahalalel, Jared, [3]Enoch, Methuselah, Lamech, Noah.

[4]The sons of Noah:
Shem, Ham and Japheth.
The Japhethites

[5]The sons of Japheth:
Gomer, Magog, Madai, Javan, Tubal, Meshek and Tiras.

[6]The sons of Gomer:
Ashkenaz, Riphath and Togarmah.

[7]The sons of Javan:
Elishah, Tarshish, the Kittites and the Rodanites.
The Hamites

[8]The sons of Ham:
Cush, Egypt, Put and Canaan.

[9]The sons of Cush:
Seba, Havilah, Sabta, Raamah and Sabteka.
The sons of Raamah:
Sheba and Dedan.

[10]Cush was the father of
Nimrod, who became a mighty warrior on earth.

[11]Egypt was the father of
the Ludites, Anamites, Lehabites, Naphtuhites, [12]Pathrusites,
Kasluhites (from whom the Philistines came) and Caphtorites.

[13]Canaan was the father of
Sidon his firstborn, and of the Hittites, [14]Jebusites, Amorites,
Girgashites, [15] Hivites, Arkites, Sinites, [16] Arvadites, Zemarites
and Hamathites.
The Semites

[17]The sons of Shem:
Elam, Ashur, Arphaxad, Lud and Aram.
The sons of Aram:
Uz, Hul, Gether and Meshek.

[18]Arphaxad was the father of Shelah,
and Shelah the father of Eber.

[19]Two sons were born to Eber:
One was named Peleg, because in his time the earth was
divided; his brother was named Joktan.

[20]Joktan was the father of
Almodad, Sheleph, Hazarmaveth, Jerah, [21]Hadoram, Uzal,
Diklah, [22]Obal, Abimael, Sheba, [23]Ophir, Havilah and Jobab.
All these were sons of Joktan.

[24]Shem, Arphaxad, Shelah,

[25]Eber, Peleg, Reu,

[26]Serug, Nahor, Terah

[27]and Abram (that is, Abraham).
The Family of Abraham

[28]The sons of Abraham:
Isaac and Ishmael.

And this listing of genealogies goes on for eight-and a-half more
chapters!

Why was there a need to trace the human bloodline back to Adam?
Why such a meticulous biblical record of the flow of humanity from the

first human man? It was to establish the traceable lineage of the coming Messiah, the kinsman redeemer prophesied during the pronouncement of cursing and judgment back in Genesis 3:15. These genealogical records exist for one purpose and one purpose only: to establish that there existed a dual bloodline in humanity, bequeathed in the Garden of Eden—the seed of Adam, being the "pure human bloodline," and the seed of Nachash, the bloodline of "mixed human and Elohim blood," as bred into Eve. And, as I noted above in the 1 Chronicles passage, the firstborn son, Cain, as well as the younger twin whom he murdered, are both omitted from the genealogy. Why? Cain is the firstborn and by Hebrew tradition should have appeared on the list immediately following Adam, but he is omitted from the genealogical record as listed in the Old Testament for the simple reason that he was not of pure, human blood. Cain was of the mixed blood of Nachash and Eve. He was the first of the Nephilim. Abel wasn't listed in the record for the simple fact that he was murdered by Cain before he had bequeathed any children. That is why we see the third third-born son, Seth, listed in the genealoical record as the direct descendent of Adam.

Again, if you recall—and this is extremely important to understand the entirety of the Old Testament—Cain, as the firstborn son of Eve, was fathered by Nachash, the Serpent character in Eden who was of the Elohim, the bright, shining prince of heaven. He represents the mixed bloodline, and if the Messiah was to be the kinsman redeemer, the savior of mankind born of mankind, his lineage had to be established as being of the pure, human bloodline, therefore, a descendent of Seth, not Cain.

The Kinsman Redeemer

The ancient Hebrew sense of redemption was firmly fixed in the word *goel* [גֹּאֵ֫ל], the act of redeeming as a kinsman. The Hebrew sensibility understood the Messiah to be the "kinsman redeemer," the one who would come to save, redeem, and rectify, but who was also a near kinsman to the family.

The concept of the kinsman redeemer was structured like this: The Law of Moses made provision for instances when a person who was forced to sell part of his property or himself into slavery, that his nearest of kin could step in and come to his aid by "buying back" what his relative was forced to sell, whether goods or person. The kinsman redeemer became the benefactor, the person who frees the enslaved by paying the ransom price and eliminating his debt.

> "If a fellow countryman of yours becomes so poor he has to sell part of his property, then his nearest kinsman is to come and buy back what his relative has sold."
> (Leviticus 25:25)

It was generally the nearest of kin who had the responsibility of redeeming his kinsman. If a person sold himself into slavery—or was forced into such—his kinsman redeemer purchased his freedom. When debt threatened to overwhelm a person, the kinsman redeemer stepped in to buy his homestead and let the family live. If a family member died without an heir, the kinsman redeemer gave his name by marrying the widow and rearing the existing son or a new son to carry on his dead relative's name. When death by murder came at the hands of another man, the kinsman redeemer acted as the avenger of blood and pursued the murderer to enact familial vengeance or bring to justice (Numbers 35:12–34; Deuteronomy 19:1–3).

So when you think of the Jewish Messiah, remember that the Hebrew concept of Messiah was the kinsman redeemer—the one who was from "among us" coming to "save or redeem us." And although this is a high, mighty biblical concept of redemption and salvation, it is also the theology in which was buried the encoded message of race interrupted and a dual human bloodline. Piggybacked on the prophecies of the coming Messiah, whose heritage was said over and over and over again throughout the Old Testament to be that of a kinsman who would be of pure human blood, was the story of a pure-blooded race versus a mixed-blood race. When the very first prophecy of the kinsman redeemer was uttered, directly after the impregnation of Eve by both Adam and Nachash, dovetailing with the proclamation that there would forever be a state of conflict between the seed of Nachash and the seed of the woman, there was a necessity to provide a traceable heritage from which the future, prophesied Messiah would be able to hail.

In short, the Old Testament story of the Messiah, and the corresponding genealogical records substantiating a traceable, pure human bloodline, obviate the complete opposite: that there was an "impure" bloodline, that which was not completely human. That was the bloodline of Nachash, the Serpent of the Garden of Eden, member of the Divine Council, one of the gods of the pantheon of gods known as the Sons of God, the *bene ha ʿElohim,* the Watchers.

I have to state emphatically that the story and prophecies of the Messiah woven throughout the entirety of the Old Testament were there for one reason: to provide an encoded, deeply subtextual message speaking to common events that every other ancient religion wrote about. The story of the coming Messiah seems more and more to simply be the Hebrew religion's collective mythology that needed to establish a pure, human bloodline. And even the "subtext of race interrupted" has dubious origins, as there is simply no way to establish any sort of solid fact. The story of the Messiah that was to come, and the genealogical record by which his human heritage was to be established, was the vehicle that was incorporated to establish a pure, human bloodline, in opposition to the bloodline that was somehow tainted. Is this a story of extraterrestrial interference? Or is it a story of the anthropological development of comparative religions? Or is it a story of the One, True God's creation and control of that which He created?

Comparatively Speaking...

The symbolic Tree of the Knowledge of Good and Evil as depicted in the Genesis account of Eden—the object of the forbidden fruit consumed by the first couple inciting God's wrath and judgment—is the Hebrew correspondent to the very same palm tree in Ea-Den, depicted as having a trunk around which a half-man-half-snake is entwined. It is from this tree that the Enki/Ea passed on knowledge and intelligence to humans—or, in the parallel Genesis scenario, Nachash taught the first human couple to partake of the forbidden knowledge. As the information was absorbed by Eve and passed on to Adam, their perceptions and awareness of reality quickly shifted, leaving the two in a severe state of shock and fear. (Author's Note: A person who is totally unaware of the reality in which he or she lives is said to reside in an "Edenic state.") The account goes on to explain that, soon thereafter, the couple ran and hid themselves from the voice of God, not because they had their first sexual experiences, nor that they were shy of their nakedness; even though Adam said they were hiding because they were naked, it was because they were suddenly, appallingly aware that there was a profound physical difference between the gods and themselves. They also were experiencing an enlightenment—for good or ill—that they had not known prior to these events. It is clear that until this time, the humans had no concept that they were in any way physically different from their reptilian/god counterparts. They had finally leapt from their childlike innocence and ignorance into the realization that they were intended, by design, to be tillers of the field and slaves to their overlords. There was also the fear, as is accounted in Genesis, that they had, as slaves who transgressed the law, brought down upon themselves the enormity of consequence.

The symbolism of the forbidden tree in Eden is not limited to Judeo-Christianity. The Eastern Indian god Krishna sat atop a coiled serpent beneath the branches of the Banyan Tree, and from there bestowed spiritual knowledge to humanity. Further representation of the tree can be found in the many crucifixion accounts of great teachers and gods, such as that of Quetzalcoatl, the winged serpent god of the great Toltec and Aztec civilization whose crucifixion on a tree is etched forever in stone. The wooden crucifixes upon which those that bestowed knowledge upon humankind—the symbols of the supreme god called the Egyptian Tau and Ahnk—represent the Tree of the Knowledge of Good and Evil. It was the result of the teaching of the forbidden knowledges to humans that they were killed.

The remarkable fact is that throughout all ancient and modern civilizations, the serpent, snake, or dragon bestowing knowledge upon the human race figures prominently in all religions and histories. The Judeo-Christian serpent as embodied in the fallen angel known as Lucifer; the Mayan serpent God Quetzalcoatl; the enormous plumed serpent god of the Hopi Indians, Baholinkonga; the mystical, human-like reptilians known as Nagas of India; the Egyptian serpent god, Kneph; the Phoenicians Agathodemon, and even the Hebrews Nakhushtan, the Brazen Serpent that Moses raised on a pole for the people to be healed—these are but a few of the myriad accounts that exist in worldwide religious cultures describing early gods as having reptilian-human physical features as well as having descended from the stars in the heavens.

Where's the Beef...?

After reading to this point, you may be asking yourself, "So, what's the 'Reptilian' connection to ancient man?" It is clear that, though our most familiar biblical stories have connectivity with ancient religions, it is also clear that there is symbolism that carries from one to the other. Not only is it my (secularized) contention that, anthropologically speaking, the Hebrew religion (aka Christianity) has its roots in language and characters modified from more ancient religions, it also carries over symbolism and adapted meanings. The importance of drawing the comparisons between the ancient Sumerian culture and the ancient Hebrew scriptural accounts is superficial in this book, at best, for there are literal tome-filled libraries speaking to these matters, but it speaks to the foundational concepts that flow throughout the religious mythologies that have given us the foundations of what we believe. The bigger question to ask is whether we are putting our faith in something that we hold to be truth, when in fact it is nothing more than accumulated myth upon myth upon myth.

Now, before you cluck your tongue in disgust at this, I must again state emphatically that faith is a completely other matter. Faith is the "substance of things hoped for, the evidence of things not seen," so said the Apostle Paul (Hebrews 11:1). Faith is the adhesive that binds together the things that don't always make sense. If you are willing to step outside the box, if only for a bit, in order to look back in and ask some serious questions, you may just find that there are other things beyond the scope of religious dogma and systematic theology. You may even step back into the box with a stronger sense of what you believe, for it's the repeated tearing down of muscle that builds its strength. The late physicist Richard Feynman put it this way:

> If you expected science to give all the answers to the wonderful questions about what we are, where we are going, what the meaning of the universe is, I think you can easily become disillusioned and then look for some mystic answer to these problems…. We're exploring, we're trying to find out as much as we can about the world!
>
> …[I]f there's a simple ultimate law that explains everything, so be it. That'd be a very nice discovery. If it turns out it's like an onion with millions of layers…then that's the way it is!… [W]hen we go to investigate we shouldn't pre-decide what it is we are trying to do except to find out more about it…. [W]e

should look to see what's true and what may not be true. Once you start doubting—which…to me, is a very fundamental part of my soul—to doubt and to ask…it gets a little harder to believe.

…I can live with doubt, uncertainty and not knowing. I think it's much more interesting to live not knowing than to have answers which might be wrong. I have approximate answers, possible beliefs, and different degrees of certainty about different things but I'm not absolutely sure of anything… But I don't have to know an answer…. I don't feel frightened by not knowing things, by being lost in the mysterious universe without having any purpose—which is the way it really is as far as I can tell….[2]

So, with my decidedly middle-of-the-road approach to personal faith, let's look at some of the comparatives in religion that seem to paint a bigger picture, not only of humanity but of the influences of the "secret history" of the Reptilians, which you will soon find isn't really a secret at all. It's just forgotten and buried in the dust of time.

Chapter Three

Coiled Around Many Cultures

"If the account given in Genesis is really true, ought
we not, after all, to thank this serpent? He was the first
schoolmaster, the first advocate of learning, the first
enemy of ignorance, the first to whisper in human ears
the sacred word, 'liberty.'"
—Robert Green Ingersoll, American statesman, 1833–1899

"Look like the innocent flower, but be the serpent under
it."

—William Shakespeare

There is a huge difference between approaching the issue of the multicultural serpent with a broad view that religion is most often a thing that cannot be quantified to the liking of the skeptical or scientific mind, versus the brand of angry atheism tantamount to hatred of any form of religion. To most skeptical thinkers and the crusading scientific atheists of today, faith is a list of pieties and practices that consist of superstitions built on the misty nothingness of ignorance and the dangerous falsehoods of faith-based thinking. (I had one scientist refer to me, in an open debate, as an "ass-plucking, denialist Nephilimer.") With this sort of eliminatory thinking, there is no room for the wonder of the spiritual (at least not openly admitted) and very little grasp of the way the theological incorporates critical thinking, let alone the complex phenomenology of the religious experience. Hardcore atheists are to religious believers what an office-bound, short-sleeved, horn-rimmed-spectacle-wearing, white shirt, and tied accountant is to the free styling, caution-to-the-wind, dreadlocked, barefooted, multi-colored-paint-smeared, loft-dwelling artist. Pardon my stereotypes.

Religion is the construct of human beings. It is the attempt to place structure on the unstructured spiritual experience, and more often than not, the foundational religious constructs evolve into a systematic set of dogmas and theologies that produce, in nearly every case, a meticulous mode of control, which bears little resemblance to the origin of the systemized structure. Spiritual experience is rarely ever something that is corporate. It is individual. That individual, in turn, internalizes and personally pursues his particular religion or, as is evident throughout the history of humanity, he moves that personal experience to a place of revelation that of necessity should be shared with those around him. But many times, the seeking of like-minded followers turns heinously into sycophancy, and the establishment of a controlled system is imposed that resembles nothing of the original experiencer's spirituality. Religion contains within its symbols and myths, some of the most utterly profound truths of the human psyche, and even the body. But these are things that need to be properly interpreted and freed from the illusion of faith and theology in order to function. Though faith is a thing that is necessary in most religious practices, it is also the thing that, in its simplicity, can completely obliterate the open mind.

Now, see? I've turned the entire argument on its head: Science and skepticism have closed off the possibilities under the lock and key of quantifiability within a "theological" approach to methodology and evidentiary research. On the other hand, "Faith-ers," in opening themselves to internalizing external spiritual experience and structuring it into theology of any sort, have adopted the rigidity that comes with legalizing their acceptance of that which is unquantifiable. It's a nasty catch-22 of thinking, so that neither approach seems to be complete, but always lacking what the other brings to the table. Science needs faith and faith needs science, and both need skepticism. Both are incomplete without the other, and that is the great schism of the mind.

The symbolism and presence of the serpent in the ancient world was highly significant, and somewhere back there, a person, a priest, or a collective of both determined that the serpent was a symbol that should be held in high esteem. Whether it was like the cat my friend and I experienced on our Sunday morning philosophical excursions, or simply a recognition that the serpent bore physical qualities that superstitiously became spiritual ones, the deifying of this reptilian creature became widespread throughout human civilization, and carried to all parts of the world. Ancient societies and religious scriptures from the Cradle of Civilization to the Far East and European cultures are rife with serpent figures, which were simultaneously attributed two highly symbolic roles: One role connected serpents to the heavens in their representation as deities, creative powers, and healing entities; the second role linked them with the underworld, associating them with darkness, evil, harm, and destructive influences. Nowadays, if one just stops and considers, there should be little difficulty recognizing this dual symbolism, as it persists, perhaps not to the same theological depths it once did, but it is there nonetheless. Look simply to the symbol of the healing serpent as it appears on the physician's caduceus, the two coiled serpents wrapped around the tree, while at the same time, we see the serpent as a thing to be feared and reviled, a representative of evil intent and even as a descriptor for wily, despicable character attributes: "That dude's a snake in the grass!"

No matter what your religious take may be on the serpent, it is clear that nearly every civilization either deified the serpent in one form or another, or looked upon the serpent as somehow sacred or symbolic of the more esoteric values in life and nature. The serpent's dualism in the Hebrew religion is clearly seen when Moses, the giver of the Law and traditional author of the Pentateuch (Genesis, Exodus, Leviticus, Numbers, and Deuteronomy), writes of the Serpent in the Garden of Eden as the seducer of Eve and the catalyst for the spiritual fall of humanity, yet upholds the serpent as the symbol of divine healing when the people are smitten by venomous snakes:

> [5]And the people spake against God, and against Moses, Wherefore have ye brought us up out of Egypt to die in the wilderness? for there is no bread, neither is there any water; and our soul loatheth this light bread. [6]And the Lord sent fiery serpents among the people, and they bit the people; and much people of Israel died. [7]Therefore the people came to Moses, and said, We have sinned, for we have spoken against the Lord, and against thee; pray unto the Lord, that he take away the serpents from us. And Moses prayed for the people. [8]And the Lord said unto Moses, Make thee a fiery serpent, and set it upon a pole: and it shall come to pass, that every one that is bitten, when he looketh upon it, shall live. [9]And Moses made a serpent of brass, and put it upon a pole, and it came to pass, that if a serpent had bitten any man, when he beheld the serpent of brass, he lived. (Numbers 21:5–9)

Moses casts a bronze, shining serpent, the *necoshet* [נְחֹשֶׁת], and raises it on a pole, and the people who were bitten were then instructed to look at it or touch the base of the pole to be healed of the terminal bites. Christianity, in turn, hailed to this miraculous healing event by equating the image of the brazen serpent elevated on the pole to the "lifting up," or crucifixion of Jesus Christ.

> [13]No one has ever gone into heaven except the one who came from heaven—the Son of Man. [14]Just as Moses lifted up the serpent in the desert, so the Son of Man must be lifted up, [15]that everyone who believes in him may have eternal life. (John 3:13–15)

Although we have no idea of how this was supposed to have worked, other than the claim of divine power, we also have no idea how much time passed and how many people died between conception of the divine brassy serpent, its sculpting design and casting, to final elevation on the pole. The story expounds on sacred symbolism over the sacred value of human life, the emphasis of the story demonstrating that the serpent was to be viewed as both the agent of harm *and* of healing—the bringer of death and the giver of life, perhaps paying homage to the fall of humanity, while at the same time revering the serpent as the deliverer of esoteric knowledge of the gods. The Hebrews sinned before their God and fiery serpents were sent to bite them as a divine punishment. In response, Moses crafted a bronze image of the venomous serpent, and the people were healed and ultimately spared by simply looking at it or touching the pole on which it had been erected.

The intent of the biblical passage is to illustrate that it is none other than God—Jehovah—who is the power working behind the image of the serpent. It is the paradoxical Jehovah who is at once the instigator of both death and life. And as God was so often want to do in Hebrew scriptures, He allows for—and in this case is the originator of—the deathly calamity in order to establish both his magnificent terror and beneficent grace in being the God who imposes harsh judgment as well as the God who offers a way out, salvation, and healing. To some, this may smack of a sort of divine Münchausen by proxy syndrome, but for the Hebrews, it was their God at work.

What is clear is that the Israelites were already quite familiar with images of deified serpents from their exposure to Egyptian mysticism and mythology during the four centuries they dwelled in Egypt, either as slaves or workers. And keep in mind that after 400 years, they were clearly "Egyptian-ized" in a similar way as if you are a descendent of an English-man who traveled to America on the *Mayflower* in 1620 and whose descendents remained here all those generations up until the current day, you would you be considered English by ancestry alone, but you would in actuality be completely American. Same deal with the Hebrews in Egypt.

The Hebrews were barely even Hebrews anymore. They had a vestige of their heritage kept alive in oral tradition and religious practice, but had completely forgotten who they were, as evidenced by the machinations Moses had to go through to keep convincing them that Jehovah was their God. They were Egyptians! But Moses came to lead them back to their ancestral promised land, and in the harshness of judgment, the serpent symbol is now seen by the Hebrews in its true light: a valid and important representation of their ancient god's ultimate power over life and death. Their life and death. What is established to them in the symbol of the bronze serpent is that God was the divine force behind the serpent figure. Now put *that* in your edenic pipe and smoke it.

The Snake Marsh of Eridu

When we consider the Sumerian creator god, Enki—paralleled by the neighboring Akkadian god, Ea—as being connected through both ancient and modern mythology to a place called the Snake Marsh, coupled with the fact that we have already established that Enki/Ea is a linguistic precursor to YWHW (Jehovah), the Middle East becomes the hotbed of early serpent mythology. The parallel being, of course, that Enki, the brother god to Elil the chief god of the Annunaki, was not only responsible for the creation of intelligent mankind as a slave race at the behest of Elil, but he also saw the humans' plight and led them into insurrection against the Annunaki. As we saw earlier, Enki/Ea is the prototype for the Hebrew Jehovah, and they played very similar functions as both creators and saviors. And the serpent symbolism is connected to them both.

In his fairly complex book *Deliver Me from Evil: Mesopotamian Incantations, 2500–1500 BC,* Oxford University researcher Graham Cunningham examines Sumerian tablets pre-dating the time known as the Sargonic period in ancient Mesopotamia, which extended from approximately the 22nd to the 23rd centuries BCE. During this earlier period in Sumer, there are many cuneiform tablets containing magical incantations, for both "helpful" and "harmful" divine ritual intervention. In these tablets we find there are two specific incantations associating Enki/Ea with various agents of illness—in other words, the summoning of infliction, harm, or illness on someone else. In these incantations there is a reference to the "Snake of Enki," while the other mentions "the place of the black snake in the middle of the abzu." Remember the term *abzu?*

This is the great, underworld sea on which the city of Eridu sits, and surrounding the city lies the swampy region known as the Snake Marsh, a place, according to the mythology, well-known and loved by Enki/ Ea. The incantations also mention a black dog, a horned snake, a serpent, and Enki himself. This association between Enki/Ea and harmful snakes continues well into the Old Babylonian period, and there is even one incantation directed against various snakes referred to as the two-tongued snake of abzu. Other incantations show that Enki/Ea could cure as well as cause illness (remember Moses and the brazen serpent on the pole), and there is a particular repeating phrase in the incantations saying *Ea did it, Ea undid it.* In essence: God brought catastrophe, God brought healing.

"Enmerkar and the Lord of Aratta" is a mythical Sumerian epic in which a speech is delivered by Enmerkar, the son of Mesh-ki-ang-gasher, the founder of the first dynasty of Uruk and builder of the city of Uruk. In that speech he delivers a magical incantation for the purpose of confusing the various languages of the people. Note the striking similarities to the Genesis account of the Tower of Babel:

> Once upon a time there was no snake, there was no
> scorpion,
> There was no hyena, there was no lion,
> There was no wild dog, no wolf,
> There was no fear, no terror,

Man had no rival.

In those days, the lands of Subur (and) Hamazi,

Harmony-tongued Sumer, the great land of the decrees of princeship,

Uri, the land having all that is appropriate,

The land Martu, resting in security,

The whole universe, the people in unison

To Enlil in one tongue [spoke].

(Then) Enki, the lord of abundance (whose) commands are trustworthy,

The lord of wisdom, who understands the land,

The leader of the gods,

Endowed with wisdom, the lord of Eridu,

Changed the speech in their mouths, [brought] contention into it,

Into the speech of man that (until then) had been one.[1]

Sumerian cylinder seal depicting Enki and Adapa in a marsh boat. Image made available through Wikimedia Commons.

In the Book of Genesis, God comes down to earth and confuses the languages of humanity, causing them to disperse. For some reason he did not want the humans working in a unified fashion as they were building their giant ziggurat to "reach to the heavens" (Genesis 11:14). Enki/Ea plays this very same language-dispersing role in the Sumerian version of the tale. So, again, we see the correlation between Enki/Ea and Jehovah of the Old Testament. And the serpent slithers in and out through the narratives.

On one of the many Akkadian green jasper cylinder seals, dating between 2000 and 2300 BCE, there is an impression of the god Enki/Ea in a reed-filled marshland setting, standing in a shallow draft boat constructed out of the long reeds growing in the marsh, traditional to the inhabitants of the area. It is obvious that the central figure in the boat is none other than Enki, as evidenced by the ever-present dual streams of water emerging from his shoulders and the fish leaping from those streams. The boat pictured on the cylinder is being guided through the heavily reeded marsh by two servants, both holding punting poles in their hands, while out of the water at the boat's fore and aft are fish leaping into the air, presumably greeting their creator in joyous worship. The entire setting on the cylinder is meant to evoke beauty and worshipful honor of Enki. One of the men standing in the boat with Enki is more than likely the man who never left his side, Adapa, the first human created by Enki. Adapa became the god's personal servant, baking daily fresh bread and fishing for his god's meals. In Sumerian hymns it is said of Enki that his greatest pastime was to navigate the waters of the Snake Marsh in his boat, known as the Ibex of the Abzu. It was here in the Snake Marsh that Enki is said to have lived in his mythical Sea House, which metaphorically cast its shadow over the waters of the Snake Marsh. If you visit the site of Eridu today, snakes can still be seen gliding across the surface of the water, forever reminding us why, after thousands of passing years, the place was given its name.

The harbor of ancient Eridu, with a boat carrying the statue of their patron god, Enki, as envisioned by archaeological artist Balage Balogh. Image used by permission from Balage Balogh, www.archaeologyillustrated.com.

Accordingly, in the ancient tablets, amplified to otherworldly proportions in the modern mythologies of the Annunaki found in the works of Zechariah Sitchin and others, it is said that Enki/Ea led a rebellion against his brother gods of the Annunaki, becoming the first "freedom fighter" for the human race, his base of operations being the Snake Marsh or Den of Serpents, known as Ea's Den. (We'll expand on this in greater detail in the next chapter.)

Around the World in 80 Serpents

Well, not quite 80, but when you consider all the civilizations, ancient, archaic, and modern, that revere or worship the serpent in some form, the list is staggering. World religion, cultural mythology, and archaic literature represent the serpent as having become synonymous with the act of fertility, life force, and creative power.[2] The fertility and sexual linkage is partly due to snakes being seen as figuratively phallic in form and symbolically synonymous of the male sex organ—not to mention the linkage to the Garden of Eden story of impregnation at the seduction of the Serpent character. Serpents also became associated with water and earth due to the many species of snakes that live in the water or in holes in the ground, and agriculture, as their dwellings were in the ground and amongst the roots and plants.

The ancient Chinese linked the serpent with the gods of rain, a life-giving symbol of fertility and abundance in their agrarian culture. Australia, India, North America, and Africa have all linked snakes with rain and rainbows (bringing to mind the aptly titled 1985 book by Wade Davis and subsequent motion picture, *The Serpent and the Rainbow,* exploring the voodoo, zombie, and reincarnating resurrection practices in the Caribbean), which, again, are connected with rain and ultimately agricultural fertility. Cultural symbolism of rebirth, resurrection, transformative power, immortality, and healing (as with the brazen serpent of Moses) became strong spiritual aspects of the serpent. This is linked to the serpent's seasonal shedding of its outer skin, the orborous, a natural, physical occurrence called sloughing. This became a demonstrable, natural symbolism for resurrection, eternity, and the perpetual renewal of life. In the two major world religions said to have sprouted from the loins of Abraham—Judaism and Islam—the serpent was representative of sexual desire,[3] reestablishing the sexual nature of the Garden of Eden story. Again reaffirming this idea, rabbinic tradition holds that the serpent in the Garden of Eden is illustrative of sexual passion and lustful desire.[4] I find it interesting that these symbols existed in Abrahamic religions despite the fact that most adherents to traditional Hebraic, Muslim, and Christian faiths are far removed from the notion that the interaction between the Serpent and Eve in the Garden of Eden was anything having to do with sexual encounter and transmission of forbidden knowledge.

In Hinduism, the *kundalini* is a coiled serpent that sits, metaphorically, at the base of the spine, a symbol of that residual power of pure desire and sexual passion.

The Hebrews and Sumerians have been touched on quite extensively, thus far, but let's do a brief recap, then move on to some other examples.

Israelite

The Hebrews held the serpent high as an evil presence embodied in the serpent that tempted Eve in the Garden of Eden. There are several other passages in the Old Testament and New Testament that speak to this character in other forms, both inanimate and possessing of character.

In Exodus 4, Moses is gifted with a magical staff that can turn to a serpent upon request. This was meant to be a sign of God's miraculous power when Moses went to confront the pharaoh of Egypt.

> [2]And the LORD said unto him, What is that in thine hand?
> And he said, A rod. [3]And he said, Cast it on the ground. And
> he cast it on the ground, and it became a serpent; and Moses
> fled from before it. [4]And the LORD said unto Moses, Put
> forth thine hand, and take it by the tail. And he put forth his
> hand, and caught it, and it became a rod in his hand: [5]That
> they may believe that the LORD God of their fathers, the God
> of Abraham, the God of Isaac, and the God of Jacob, hath
> appeared unto thee.
> (Exodus 4:2–5)

This very same rod-turned-serpent was a magical trick duplicated by the court magicians in Egypt, but as the story goes, Moses' rod-snake devoured the snakes produced by the Pharaoh's magicians. Again, according to Hebrew religion, a demonstration of God's power and Moses' demonstration that his snake was bigger than the Pharaoh's.

> [8]And the LORD spake unto Moses and unto Aaron, saying,
> [9]When Pharaoh shall speak unto you, saying, Shew a miracle

for you: then thou shalt say unto Aaron, Take thy rod, and cast it before Pharaoh, and it shall become a serpent. [10]And Moses and Aaron went in unto Pharaoh, and they did so as the LORD had commanded: and Aaron cast down his rod before Pharaoh, and before his servants, and it became a serpent. [11]Then Pharaoh also called the wise men and the sorcerers: now the magicians of Egypt, they also did in like manner with their enchantments. [12]For they cast down every man his rod, and they became serpents: but Aaron's rod swallowed up their rods. [13]And he hardened Pharaoh's heart, that he hearkened not unto them; as the LORD had said.
(Exodus 7:8–13)

It is biblical stories like these that cause me to ponder why an infinite God did things the way He did them. It seems that God could have simply manifested Himself to the Egyptians, demonstrating that He was, indeed, a benevolent deity, resulting in the Egyptians falling on their faces and worshipping Him. Instead, according to the story in Exodus, God marionettes His followers through a series of devastatingly awesome events that equated to nothing more than the wreaking of destruction, mayhem, and suffering, when He could simply have gained the respect, worship, and reverence by manifesting Himself to the Pharaoh and the people of Egypt. Is this a God of infinite wisdom, holiness, and omniscience, or is it the manufactured god of humans in a historically culturally driven tale? That is the big question whose theme resonates throughout the subtext of this book. But as the systematic Judeo-Christian theology dictates, "Who am I to question God's ways?" It's an issue of faith in the supernatural that became law, theology, and dogma, as we will see repeated throughout many ancient religions.

If some of what I write seems as if I have some sort of axe to grind with biblical theology, please do not misinterpret me. What you see here are the shards of traditional stories *not* being filtered through religious predisposition, but the tales as seen from outside the box of dogma.

When you look at these stories in that light, they become less God-inspired accounts and more of the same sort of religious mythological transference of divinity-driven theology for the purpose of establishing a picture that the teller of tale wanted told. The symbolism used to denote divine power is demonstrated in mythical proportions in the following passages:

> 4[The Hebrews] traveled from Mount Hor along the route to the Red Sea, to go around Edom. But the people grew impatient on the way; 5they spoke against God and against Moses, and said, "Why have you brought us up out of Egypt to die in the desert? There is no bread! There is no water! And we detest this miserable food!" 6Then the Lord sent venomous snakes among them; they bit the people and many Israelites died. 7The people came to Moses and said, "We sinned when we spoke against the Lord and against you. Pray that the Lord will take the snakes away from us." So Moses prayed for the people. 8The Lord said to Moses, "Make a snake and put it up on a pole; anyone who is bitten can look at it and live. 9So Moses made a bronze snake and put it up on a pole. Then when anyone was bitten by a snake and looked at the bronze snake, he lived."
> (Number 21:4–9)

> 11"Beware that thou forget not the Lord thy God, in not keeping his commandments, and his judgments, and his statutes, which I command thee this day.... 15Who led thee through that great and terrible wilderness, wherein were fiery *serpents* (author's emphasis), and scorpions, and drought, where there was no water; who brought thee forth water out of the rock of flint..." (Deuteronomy 8:11,15)

As we have already examined, the serpent that Moses cast in bronze, many years later, became on object of worship itself. The nehushtan, as it was called (a derivative of the word *Nachash*), had taken on the status of god, and a cult formed around its worship, so much so that King Hezekiah expurgated the cult and tore down the bronze serpent. Apparently, serpent worship in Jerusalem was not new in Israel, as there are no less than seven such bronze serpents from pre-Israelite Palestinian cities. Two of these serpents were uncovered during an archaeological dig at Megiddo,[5] one at the ancient cite of Gezer,[6] two from the "holy of holies" at the ruins of Hazor, and another two at the remains Shechem.[7] There are several other archaeological discoveries of the snake and serpent in the Canaanite region, but they mostly predate Israel's occupation of the territory. However, with what we understand of the spread of religion and the adaptations from culture to culture, it is clear that the Israelites simply appropriated the older Palestinian serpent worship, blending it with their own version of serpent worship as embodied in the bronze serpent of Moses.

It is interesting to note that despite all the miraculous wonders experienced by the Hebrews under the leadership of Moses, and during the great exodus from Egypt, the people still clung to the physical objects such as the golden calf and the serpent, and elevated them to the status worthy of their worship. Could this be some indicator as to what really happened in these biblical tales? Ask yourself: Would you, if confronted with the sea splitting open to allow you to pass on dry ground, or if you stood before the fiery mountain where Moses ascended to receive the tablets, or if you experienced all the other miraculous wonders of the Hebrew's 40-year sojourn in the desert, forget about what God performed and worship an idol!? Or, perhaps, the Hebrews never really experienced any of these things on the same level as they have been passed down to us in biblical religious myth. Perhaps the experiencer, Moses, constructed an elaborate religion from the bare bones of personal divine revelation, but the hard part for him was convincing the people to live by the dictates of his individual encounter with a god. And then, in a posthumous slap in the face to Moses, throughout the next few hundred years, the people took his brazen serpent on a pole, incorporated it into Canaanite religion of Palestine, and began worshipping the snake as if it were the God of their deliverance.

¹Now it came to pass in the third year of Hoshea son of Elah king of Israel, that Hezekiah the son of Ahaz king of Judah began to reign. ²Twenty and five years old was he when he began to reign; and he reigned twenty and nine years in Jerusalem. His mother's name also was Abi, the daughter of Zachariah. ³And he did that which was right in the sight of the Lord, according to all that David his father did. ⁴He removed the high places, and brake the images, and cut down the groves, and brake in pieces the brasen *serpent* (author's emphasis) that Moses had made: for unto those days the children of Israel did burn incense to it: and he called it Nehushtan.
(2 Kings 18:1–4)

In magnificent poetic form, Job 26: 6–14 presents a picture of God's handiwork. The serpent is mentioned near the end of the passage:

⁶"Death is naked before God;
Destruction lies uncovered.

⁷He spreads out the northern [skies] over empty space;
he suspends the earth over nothing.

⁸He wraps up the waters in his clouds,
yet the clouds do not burst under their weight.

⁹He covers the face of the full moon,
spreading his clouds over it.

¹⁰He marks out the horizon on the face of the waters
for a boundary between light and darkness.

¹¹The pillars of the heavens quake,
aghast at his rebuke.

¹²By his power he churned up the sea;
by his wisdom he cut Rahab to pieces.

¹³By his breath the skies became fair;
his hand pierced the crooked serpent.

¹⁴And these are but the outer fringe of his works;
how faint the whisper we hear of him!
Who then can understand the thunder of his power?"

What is this "crooked serpent" spoken of in the passage? It appears again in Old Testament scripture:

> [1]In that day the LORD with His hard, great and strong sword shall visit leviathan the serpent, and leviathan, the *crooked serpent* (author's emphasis), and shall slay the whale that is in the sea. [2]In that day there shall be singing to the vineyard of pure wine. [3]"I am the Lord that keep it, I will suddenly give it drink, lest any hurt come to it, I keep it night and day."
> (Isaiah 27:1–3)

There are many interpretations of the "crooked serpent," the leviathan and dragon, ranging from a presence of the Holy Ghost, to the constellation of Draco, to a prophecy of the swastika of the Nazi regime.

In all, the serpent is mentioned more than 40 times in biblical references. An exhaustive listing here would be simply that: a list. Rather than reference every passage, suffice it to say that all you need do is refer to a Concordance of the Bible words and look under the heading for "serpent" or "snake." You could also conduct an Internet search for the words "serpent + bible," then sit back and find the voluminous Web pages and limitless amount of information and interpretation, from the scholarly to completely whack fringe. Suffice it to say that the Bible establishes the serpent mythology was at play in ancient Israel, most probably carried over, in their origins, from the Egyptian, Palestinian, and Sumerian cultures that influenced the early development of Hebrew religion.

The Great Dragon: China

For four millennia, Chinese culture has existed and thrived in an unbroken line, dating back to the Xia Dynasty as early as 2000 BCE. China's mythological roots, however, extend even farther back in time. Five thousand years ago in China, around the time the ancient Britons were building the first circular ditch and mound of Stonehenge, the dragon began its long-standing tradition as a mythological figure of the Chinese people. Unlike the serpent or snake in other cultures, the Chinese held the serpent/dragon as a symbol of happiness, immortality, sexual intercourse, and fertility, imbued with the ability to ward off evil spirits. The pervasive dragon decorates nearly every ancient monument and structure in China, as well as adorning the garments of ancient Chinese generals and high governmental officials. The Emperor wore nine dragons on his brocaded robe.

In ancient times, again illustrating the dual nature of the serpent, the dragon was regarded as not only the highest of sacred animals, but it also became the imperial emblem of all Chinese emperors. Unlike the depictions of evil dragons of Western cultures, and the need for St. Patrick to drive the evil serpents from the Land of Ireland, the Chinese dragon is beneficent and gracious among all other creatures, and was worshipped as the divine ruler of lakes, rivers, and seas. It is the powerful yet gentle serpent Lung that brings the fertile, healing rain to the earth, giving life to the crops and cooling and quenching the thirst of the toiling husbandman.

The dragon ultimately became synonymous with the Chinese, who proudly proclaim themselves "Long De Chuan Ren" (Descendents of the Dragon). The long line of emperors believed themselves to be, as did the Egyptians and other monarchical families in ancient times—the sons of heaven (the Sons of God; the Elohim), brothers to the gods, and incarnate embodiments of the sacred dragons. All the empirical accouterments became known as things that were of the dragon: The bed of the emperor was the dragon bed; the throne, the dragon seat; and the emperor's ceremonial robes, the dragon robes. The dragon was in and throughout every aspect of ceremonial worship and daily life.

For half a millennium, the Xia people and their dynasty dominated the northern regions of China, from about 2000 to 1500 BCE. They were a people who collectively worshipped the sacred serpent, a creature found coiled around the most ancient of Chinese mythologies. Through the course of religious evolution, the serpent took on the form of the traditional Chinese dragon, and became the most everlasting symbol of a people and the most recognized emblem of Chinese culture, spirituality and mythology.

In 551 BCE, a child named Kongfuzi was born into a poor family of aristocratic lineage. His family's lineage allowed him the ability to become an educator and governmental official. Better known to the world as Confucius, his philosophy as an educator was that learning, in and of itself, was the path to greater self-knowledge and self-improvement. Working for and attaining these things would lead you to good conduct and clean living. His teachings took on legendary proportion through the centuries and millennia, but his underlying goal was to make wisdom the divine force that would result in the smooth operation of a stable and well-ordered state of being. Sounds very New Age, doesn't it? As most of us know, his teachings became a legendary guide to living wisely.

Many followers flocked to the teachings of Confucius, and they continued to perpetuate his ideas, even after his death in 479 BCE. As is with most legendary figures, who attained legendary status even during their own lifetimes, legends were fostered and spread about Confucius, including one in which sacred dragons guarded his mother during her pregnancy and attended to her at his birth.

Mesoamerican Feathered Serpent

According to Aztec, Mayan, and Toltec scriptures, Quetzalcoatl, the feathered serpent god, was the primordial creator and giver of life to all that is. Along with his mirrored opposite god, Tezcotlipoca, he created the world, and he was sometimes referred to as the "White Tezcotlipoca," contrasted to his darker opposite, the god of the night. He was called the great Sky God, the "Lord of the East," being associated with the morning star, which also gave him the name Tlahuizcalpantecuhtli, "Lord of the Star of the Dawn." Quetzalcoatl was also of virgin birth, his mother being the goddess Coatlicue and his twin brother god, Xoloti, known as the evening star, associated with Venus. It was Quetzalcoatl who, after the death of the fourth sun (Fourth Age), descended to Mictlan, the land of the dead, and by sprinkling blood drawn from his penis over the bones of the dead he had gathered from the previous era, created the fifth sun and the dawning of the new age of mankind.

The Temple of the Feathered Serpent has fine stylized depictions of that deity in a style that includes the apparent influences of Teotihuacan and Maya art. Image made available through Wikimedia Commons.

Comparatively speaking, the resemblance to titles used for Jesus, the Bright Morning Star, and Lucifer [הֵילֵל], the Morning Star, are striking. This begs the question as to whether the Jesus of early Christianity garnered His title from the same sort of evolution of pagan, earth-based religious belief as did Quetzalcoatl, only a few hundred years later. Although Christianity teaches that God (the Creator) and Lucifer/Satan/Devil (the created) are not precise opposites, despite the fact that they represent opposing forces of good and evil, and that-which-is-holy versus that-which-is-profane, the dual nature of the opposing forces is present in nearly all religious belief and mythology in every culture. In this sense, Quetzalcoatl becomes the very same archetype. And because we all know that the morning and evening stars are merely a planet in the solar system, attributing them to being the presence of divinity, even on a comparative level, is certainly nothing short of an archaic understanding on the part of both religious mythologies. As humans, we have always looked to the equinoxes and the traversing of the heavenly bodies to ascribe some sort of mystical substance to our gods.

The dual, or twin, aspects of Quetzalcoatl and Xoloti is not lost on the comparison between Jesus and Lucifer, who are not only the diametrically opposing elements in the Christian faith, but also hypothesized, by some wags, to be twin brothers, both of the Elohim.

As with other gods riddled throughout human history, it was Quetzalcoatl, the feathered serpent, who—as is attributed to Lucifer, Enki/Ea, Khrisna, and others—brought the knowledge of the gods to humanity, this act bestowing on him the additional title of "wise legislator." And, as with the Serpent in the Garden of Eden, he was condemned by the other gods, and crucified on a tree, like Jesus Christ, the Messiah of the Christian faith.

Veneration of Quetzalcoatl as a god appears to have begun in the early Classic Mesoamerican periods between 400 BCE and 600 AD, and spread throughout Mesoamerica by the Late Classic Period (600–900 AD).[8] There is some credence to the academic notion that Quetzalcoatl was merely a deified earthly king from an earlier Mesoamerican period, which would also fit the picture of most mythological gods who once had firm footing in the flesh and blood, but with the evolution of legend, became much, much more.

In the Aztec culture, whose religious beliefs are among the best-documented in historical sources, Quetzalcoatl was the god of the wind, the star of the dawn, of merchants, arts, crafts, and knowledge. He was also, as the bringer of learning and knowledge, the patron god of the Aztec priesthood,[9] another cross-cultural similarity to the Illuminator and Bringer of Knowledge.

In one version of the myth, Quetzalcoatl allowed himself to be seduced by his smoking mirror opposite, Tezcatlipoca, and in his resultant remorse, threw himself on a funeral pyre, killing himself by "theocricide." After his death his heart became the morning-star, creating his identification with the god Tlahuizcalpantecuhtli. Toltec religious dualism has it that Tezcatlipoca, the opposing deity to Quetzalcoatl, had reportedly driven the god into exile. According to yet another tradition, Quetzalcoatl traveled over the sea on a raft of snakes. Quetzalcoatl has been physically described as being light-skinned and bearded, and prophesies of his future return were connected to his mythology. When the Spanish conquistador Hernán Cortés appeared in Mesoamerica in 1519, the Aztec king at the time, Montezuma II, lured by the higher technology, weaponry, and appearance of the Conquistadors, was easily convinced that Cortés was in fact the reincarnate Quetzalcoatl, returning to rule his people.

Quetzalcoatl became a dualistic serpentine symbol of death and resurrection. The god has a great affinity with the priest-king Topiltzin Ce Acatl Quetzalcoatl, who ruled the Toltecs in Tula during the 10th century. The cult of Quetzalcoatl became widespread in Teotihuacan, an area about 30 miles north of what is now Mexico City, as well as Xochilco, Cholula, and Chichen Itza.

In his book *Fingerprints of the Gods: The Evidence of Earth's Lost Civilization*, British author Graham Hancock published a controversial theory that states Egyptian culture, as well as all the Mesoamerican culture inclusive of the Aztec, Mayan, and Olmec, all shared similar Quetzalcoatl mythologies.[10] The stories of a bearded, light-skinned man bringing "knowledge" are alleged to be common, and sprouting from a central source or a "master/proto" culture. As racist as that may sound by today's standards of politically correct–speak, keep in mind that the mythologies are much older than current, 21st-century politics. The caterwaul by the scientific community is that all these theories are based on some sort of tacit racism, when in fact, it is the cultures themselves that have given us the stories, not later cultures attributing those stories to only the, as some in the scientific community call them, "brown peoples."

Native American Rattlesnake

The serpent is revered among Native American tribes in the form of the rattlesnake, who is known as "Grandfather" and "King of Snakes." It is he who gives both fair winds and is the bringer of tempestuous weather, aligning with the myths of Quetzalcoatl and his connection to the wind and weather.

In Native American Chippewa and Cherokee flood mythology, the Horned Serpent, Misiginebig, an evil, underwater serpent/dragon, kills one of the gods' cousins. In an act of divine revenge, the gods kill the Horned Serpent, who in dying unleashes a great flood. The people first flee to the mountains and when they, too, become submerged, they float on a raft of serpents until the flood subsides. The evil spirits once controlled by the serpent god then go into hiding out of fear of further punishment and repercussion. Again, the similarities to the Nephilim and the Flood of Noah are undeniable, as the Hebrew scripture tells us that the Nephilim were "on the earth in those days and also afterward" (Genesis 6:4). This is not to establish the Flood of Noah as the prototype or "true" story, but rather to compare the Flood of Noah to the other cultural accounts, demonstrating the common theme amongst varying cultural tales. (Anecdotally, in Ohio, atop a plateau overlooking the Brush Creek Valley, Serpent Mound is the largest and finest serpent effigy in the United States. The Mound Builders associated some great mystical value to the serpent, as demonstrated by archaeological cites such as the Serpent Mound, though, to date, no one has been able to decipher the particular associations.)

The Canaanite Basilik

The early, pre-Canaanite Phoenicians (the basis of the name "phoenix," the rising firebird/dragon) had a serpent god called the Basilisk (made popular in one of the *Harry Potter* books and movies). This serpent wasn't quite a serpent, but bore some of the physical characteristics of an early dragon figure, again demonstrating the migrated physicalized presence of the earlier serpentine representations. The Basilisk was considered to be an early representation of a phallic god, common in ancient religions, obviously founded in male domination. According to the mythology, to look directly at a Basilisk meant certain death in many of heinous forms, so it is impossible to picture them accurately, as no one was able to look at them and create an accurate representation. This ability to kill with a glance is shared by the gorgons of Greek mythology, mythical correspondents of the Basilisk. In turn, the only way to kill a basilisk was blindfolded and by use of indirect visual, such as by a mirror or by use of a mirror-like object in which the serpent could view its own reflection, as was the case with the Grecian myth of Perseus and his fight with Medusa.

First-century Roman historian Pliny the Elder wrote of the Basilisk: "The basilisk serpent has the same power, to kill with its gaze. It is a native of Cyrenaica, not more than 12 inches long. It routs all snakes with its hiss, and moves its body forward in manifold coils like other snakes."[11]

During the Middle Ages, the basilisk became identified with the cockatrice, a two-legged dragon with a the head of a rooster, very similar to the phoenix, a serpent mentioned occasionally in the Old Testament book of Isaiah and other Hebrew scriptures:

> And the sucking child shall play on the hole of the asp, and the weaned child shall put his hand on the cockatrice' den.
> (Isaiah 11:8)

Rejoice not thou, whole Palestina, because the rod of him that smote thee is broken: for out of the serpent's root shall come forth a cockatrice, and his fruit shall be a fiery flying serpent. (Isaiah 14:29)

They hatch cockatrice' eggs, and weave the spider's web: he that eateth of their eggs dieth, and that which is crushed breaketh out into a viper. (Isaiah 59:5)

For, behold, I will send serpents, cockatrices, among you, which will not be charmed, and they shall bite you, saith the lord. (Jeremiah 8:17)

When we enter the modern period, and Medusa becomes an innocuous decorative motif found on door knockers and broaches, the Basilisk immigrates to the United States and becomes identified with different American snakes, most notably the rattlesnake. One of the first rattlesnakes encountered by European explorers, a tropical variety known as the "Mexican West Coast rattlesnake," was given the scientific name *crotalus basiliscus,* or "Basilisk snake."

(On an interesting etymological note, the work *Basilisk* is where we got the later word for a temple of the phallic god, and eventually a type of church: the *basilica.* There is a remembrance to this ancient mythology found atop St. Peter's Basilica in Rome in the form of a phallic ball.)

Hindu Mythology

The worship of snakes and serpents in Hindu culture and religion demonstrates high status of snakes or nagas, in their mythology. नाग is the Sanskrit and Pāli word for a deity or class of entity or being, taking the form of a very large snake, found in Hinduism and Buddhism. The use of the term *naga* is often ambiguous, as the word may also refer, in similar contexts, to one of several human tribes known as or nicknamed the Nāgas. The term is still used to apply to ordinary snakes, particularly the King Cobra and the Indian Cobra, the latter of which is still called naga in Hindi and other languages of India.

The serpent primarily represents symbolic rebirth, death, and mortality, again as we've seen in other cultures, due to the casting of its skin and symbolic "rebirth." Carved representations of cobras or nagas can be found all across India, to which offerings of food and flowers are left, with lights burned before the many and various shrines. Among some South Indians, the cobra is so revered that, if accidentally killed, it is burned like a human being on a funerary pyre; no one would kill one intentionally.

The Serpent Nāgas form an important part of Hindu mythology and play prominent roles in various legends. The following is a list of serpents from Hindu mythology[12]:

Shesha (Adisesha, Sheshnaga, or the 1,000-headed snake) upholds the world on his many heads and is said to be used by Lord Vishnu to rest. Shesha also sheltered Lord Krishna from a thunderstorm during his birth.

Vasuki allowed himself to be coiled around Mount Mandara by the Devas and **Asuras** to churn the milky ocean creating the ambrosia of immortality.

Kaliya poisoned the Yamuna/Jamuna River where he lived. Krishna subdued Kaliya by dancing on him and compelled him to leave the river.

Manasa is the queen of the snakes. She is also referred to as Manasha or "Ma Manasha," with *ma* being the universal mother.

Ananta is the endless snake who circles the world.

Padmanabha (or Padmaka) is the guardian snake of the south.

Astika is half-Brahmin and half-naga.

Kulika.

Lord Shiva also wears a snake around his neck.

An important Hindu festival bearing ancient association with snake worship is *Nag panchami*. It is held on the fifth day of Shravana, and snake idols are offered gifts of milk and incense. It is said that the gaining of wisdom, wealth, and fame are sought after by the offering of milk and incense to the serpent idol. Once again, the serpent is associated with illumination and the getting of knowledge.

Egyptian

Apophis, also known as Apep,[13] dating back into the 1500s BCE, was the great water serpent god who slept in the mountains of Baku, rising with the morning star, daily attacks Ra on his journeys through the daytime sky and the underworld, and is subsequently destroyed each evening by Sobek, the god of the crocodiles.

As we have seen in most other religions and cultures thus far, the serpent seems to always hold some chthonic symbolism—that underworld characterization as the giver of life, possessing the creator aspect that seems ever present wherever the serpent is worshipped. Nowhere is this so evident and pervasive than in the mysticism of ancient Egyptian religion and worship. In the mythology and symbolism of Egypt exist some of the most glaring dualistic contrasts between reverent worship of the serpent and fear-based repudiation.

The Egyptians' reverence for the serpent's life-giving powers probably arose, in part, from—once again—observing them shedding their skins, continually exposing a new resurrected body in the process. The god Atum, the ancient Egyptian primeval creator deity, is represented in the form of the serpent who seasonally shed his outer skin, a symbol of the continual life, death, and new life cycle. At one point, Atum prophesies to Osiris, the Egyptian god of the netherworld and final judgment, that he is going to destroy the entire world he had created and revert back to his serpentine form.[14]

Early-20th-century Dutch-born archaeologist Henri Frankfort, who spent his life reconstructing ancient Egyptian and Mesopotamian culture and mythology, said of the Egyptian serpent gods, "The primeval snake survives when everything else is destroyed at the end of time. Thus the serpent was strongly and continually associated with creation and eternal existence in the ancient Egyptian ethos. The Egyptians portrayed life itself by the image of the rearing serpent, and a serpent biting its tail was a common Egyptian emblem for 'eternity.'"[15]

During the Egyptian Middle Kingdom (2030–1640 BCE), post-11th Dynasty, the god Amun came onto the scene as the patron god of the capitol city of Thebes. Amun in one of his manifestations was that of the serpent god named Kematef ("he who has completed his time").[16] At Karnak, during the beginning of the New Kingdom (1550–1090 BCE), Amun was merged with the sun god Ra, when Pharaoh Ahknaten uprooted the entire Egyptian system of religion and worship and decreed a new, monotheistic society. "Amun-Ra became the monotheistic, supreme state-enforced/endorsed god of Egypt during this period. Amun-Ra's divine consort, the serpent goddess Mut ("the resplendent serpent") gave birth to a son named Khonsu."[17] Together, this holy triad, in the Egyptian worldview, symbolized the perfect union both in the house of the gods as well as being representative of the supreme social structure of the royal family. And it was this family portrait that inextricably linked the house and family of the pharaoh to the mythological serpent of Egyptian mythology. But Ahkenaten's monotheistic society lasted but one generation before it was overthrown and the implementation of a reversion back to the polytheism took place.

All periods of Egyptian history, from the earliest historical times all the way to the end of the New Kingdom, creation, fertility, birth, the goodness of the gods, rebirth, and resurrection were all embodied in the image of the serpent. Thermuthis was the serpent-headed goddess to whom were brought offerings at the time of harvest, thanking her for successful crops of both food and grape of the vine.[18]

The Father of Serpents, Geb, was the god of earth and "the father of the gods."[19] The snake was linked to life after death and the recurring cycle of life due to Egyptian obsession with the quest for eternal life, and he became a symbol of survival after death and even resurrection among the ancient Egyptians. In the *Egyptian Book of the Dead*, sometimes referred to by its more precise title, *The Book of Going Forth by Day*, in chapter 87, we are told that transformation into a serpent upon death gives new life to the deceased.[20]

A serpent goddess in pre-dynastic Egypt set the stage for her veneration as an enduring symbol throughout the rest of dynastic Egyptian history. The most important serpent of Lower Egypt was Wadjet ("the green one") who eventually became the symbol of a unified Egypt and its royal house. It was this serpent goddess whose name became synonymous with the general Egyptian term for *cobra* and the foundation for the creation of the symbol of the uraeus, the standing figure of the cobra found most often as the headpiece on the royal Egyptian crowns. The cobra/uraeus became such an important piece of Egyptian iconography that the life of the Pharaoh became known as the living years of the uraeus.[21] Wadjet not only became physically represented on the Pharaoh's crown as his guardian and protector, but eventually was bestowed the title of the Eye of Ra. Her green color, significantly, became the color that represented resurrection in ancient Egypt, and Wadjet, also referred to as "the green one," embodied the forces of health and fertility. As with most gods out of antiquity, you can quickly see how numerous titles continued to be added on, as the powers and influence of the god evolved in worship (Wadjet: the green uraeus of the Pharaoh, the Eye of Ra, the protector and guardian of the life of the Pharaoh, the power of fertility and good health).

The crown of 18th-Dynasty Egypt, clearly showing the serpent figure. Copyright Sirius Project, Dr. John Ward, and Dr. Maria Nilsson, Luxor, Egypt. Used by permissioon of the Sirius Project.

Representing the oppositional character of the Egyptian serpent was the Serpent God of Darkness, the winged, fire-spewing Apophis, What Wadjet was to all that was good in ancient Egypt, Apophis was her counterpart, representing the demonic forces, evil gods, and powers of the bleak underworld. Apophis was the serpent of darkness, in complete opposition to the sun god Ra, who was the light of the world. But Apophis, albeit the antithesis to Ra, was never more powerful. He simply counterbalanced the serpent Mehen ("the coiled one") who was the protector of the sun god Ra, assisting him on his journey through the realm of night to be reborn every morning.[22] And as you find in many cultures and religions, the powers of darkness are thwarted by the power of good. As Satan is to God, so Apophis is to Ra, with minor alterations to the functionality.

It has been said time and again that the ancient Egyptians were utterly preoccupied with death—at least the royal family's, as far as can be seen. Their entire lives, especially when a seated Pharaoh, were consumed with the afterlife and the resurrection. There is an interesting entry in the Pyramid Texts, the funerary papyri of ancient Egypt. In these documents is listed something for which there is very little explanation: the "snake game,"[23] presumably a test of sorts, played out in the afterlife when a Pharaoh died—a game he has to win. How interesting a tie to modern Christinaity would that be!? The notion of an Egyptian judgment, test, or fist-a-cuff in order to enter the beautiful wonders of the afterlife seem a colloquial version of a much greater religious prime.

The Gadsen Flag: "Don't Tread on Me." Image copyright of the author.

Don't Tread on Me

Being an American and a citizen of the United States, I cannot overlook the serpent symbolism in some of my country's own iconography, continuing a long tradition of the snake making its appearance in the cultures of humanity. The Gadsen Flag, commonly recognized as the yellow "Don't Tread on Me" banner, emblazoned with the coiled rattlesnake, was named after Christopher Gadsen, a colonial general and statesman. Benjamin Franklin wrote of the rattlesnake as a symbol for American vigilance:

> I recollected that her eye excelled in brightness, that of
> any other animal, and that she has no eye-lids—She may
> therefore be esteemed an emblem of vigilance. She never
> begins an attack, nor, when once engaged, ever surrenders: She
> is therefore an emblem of magnanimity and true courage.—As
> if anxious to prevent all pretensions of quarreling with her, the
> weapons with which nature has furnished her, she conceals in
> the roof of her mouth, so that, to those who are unacquainted
> with her, she appears to be a most defenseless animal; and even
> when those weapons are shewn and extended for her defense,
> they appear weak and contemptible; but their wounds however
> small, are decisive and fatal:—Conscious of this, she never
> wounds till she has generously given notice, even to her enemy,
> and cautioned him against the danger of stepping on her.—Was
> I wrong, Sir, in thinking this a strong picture of the temper and
> conduct of America?[24]

The serpent has always been associated with strength and influence, despite its dualism as both a creature to be feared and revered. It can be asserted, however, that given such overwhelming evidence from texts and inscriptions, the ultimate duality in nature and perception of the serpent was illustrated by the need to have the serpent demonstrably enact both supreme goodness as well as ultimate evil among the ancient Egyptians, and that serpent imagery was incontrovertibly associated with the afterlife, resurrection, and eternity, as with so many other serpents in so many other religions and cultures.

The Serpent in Alien Subculture

Chapter Four

The Reptoids...Reptilians—No, Wait... Reptilian-Humanoids

As you have seen, the key to understanding the connectivity of the serpent to Reptilian/alien mythos is completely predicated on having an understanding of how the serpent's role became so important in human history—more specifically, to people, themselves. Believe what you will about spirituality, religion, science, or anthropology, the serpent figure has played prominently in the lore of ancient theory, and has become the rock star of current alien conspiratorial thought, the theory itself becoming the "mother ship" for all the varied, extraneously divergent sub-theories making the rounds in the circles of the ufological faithful. Make no mistake: The secret history of the Reptilians is as much a manufactured "religion" as are the snake and dragon cults from the depths of our anthropological past. That does not mean they do not exist in some form. If that was the final conclusion, this book would end right here.

The Bacilica of Reptilica

Gnosticism will tell you that the truest sense of theology is psychology. I would add anthropology to that mix—and that claims made about God or gods, are in their truest sense, actually only projections of humanity, the reflections of who we deem ourselves to be. After all, religion is humankind's attempt to fill the god-shaped vacuum that exists in the human mind and heart, creating and re-creating God in the form that we need Him to be; religion, of course, being something completely different than spirituality—certainly on the same chart, just a different emphasis. We project and extrapolate our needs onto what we think God should be, and—*viola!*—we have religion.

What is all this talk about religion doing in a section of the book that is supposed to be about Reptilian/alien subculture, one might ask? Intrinsically, it is because they are the *very same thing*. Humans have some deep primordial, psychological, physiological wiring that makes us want to know more about who we are and where we come from and where we are supposed to go from there. Human beings have an innate need to know our roots, and discover the reasons we are what we are and why we do what we do, but then we incorporate our innate creativity to construct the landscape around us. We can take the minutest of causality and convert that to consequence, and in so doing, we may find ourselves constructing a psychological fortress that will house and protect the way we conceive our universe and interact with our surroundings. So let's take a brief jaunt into the psychology of the need for God and aliens and everything else in between. Those base needs sprout from the human psyche.

To get some grasp of why the mind works the way it does in regard to these matters of mythology, let's take a simple look to the "fathers" of modern psychology: Sigmund Freud and Alfred Adler.

Freud, although a pioneer in his field—some of whose ideas have been left behind as we learn more and more about how the mind operates—focused his research on the unconscious/subconscious mind and how it juggles innate biological motives that are hardwired into human physiology, alongside the brain's ability to produce irrational thinking. Repressed, early memories were at the root of what Freud was looking for, and he referred to his methods as *depth psychology,* a going back to our roots to see what we're made of and why we operate the way we do in the current. We hear so much about modes of operation and family systems when we are trying to root out the origins of behaviors, which ultimately was fleshed out for the first time with Freud's research. This brand of looking-to-the-past-psychology *can* be applied corporately (to a group), but Freud was much more interested in how the *individual* formed these modes prior to cognitive awareness.

On the other hand, common sense and conscious behavior were the focus of Adler's research, leading him to emphasize what he called *surface* or *context psychology.* He believed that cognitive social motives and intimate social interactions were what drove behaviors in people, and he was aptly dubbed the father of ego and humanistic psychology. His work in cognitive and family therapy led him to the conclusion that it was the interactive social structure between people[1]—especially family members—that was the primary motivation for human behavior. The goal for Adler's form of therapy was to focus on a form of daily living experience that made social interaction the primary focus.

Freud, generally speaking, filtered his view of human nature through a pessimistic view of the things that govern behavioral outcomes. He adhered to a Darwinian/Hobbesian philosophy, which basically states that man in the state of nature, according to Hobbes, has no idea of moral goodness, and therefore must be naturally wicked; he is vicious because he does not know virtue. Throw a little "survival of the fittest" into the mix, and you have the rudimentary basics of Darwinian-Hobbesian Theory. (Hold on, psychologists; I'm going somewhere with all of this.)

Adler had a much more optimistic approach to the foundations of cognitive behavior, following a more or less Rousseau-ian/Humanistic philosophy, which espoused that human nature is innately good, and that society, our surrounding, and environment are the corrupting force that transforms man into self-interested/self-actualizing people.

> The first man who, having fenced in a piece of land, said
> "This is mine," and found people naïve enough to believe
> him, that man was the true founder of civil society. From how
> many crimes, wars, and murders, from how many horrors and
> misfortunes might not any one have saved mankind, by pulling
> up the stakes, or filling up the ditch, and crying to his fellows:
> Beware of listening to this impostor; you are undone if you
> once forget that the fruits of the earth belong to us all, and the
> earth itself to nobody.
> —Jean Jacques Rousseau, *Discourse on Inequality*, 1754

Sense of self, Frued contended, was determined by what was passed on to you from your parents, immediate family, and social externals, such as the environmental factors of familial relations, parenting, and social interactivity that took place when we were infants and small children—as well as decisive, life-altering experiences as we grow older. We are not only influenced, but governed and manipulated by our past experiences, so in getting to the roots of who you really are and why you act in certain methods and modes of operation, you have to return to your foundations and the starting points that launched certain lifelong behaviors. Freud promoted the retracing of your steps to see where you came from, the influences of that past, and how you've gotten to where you are in the current. Your personality and present modes of operation are, therefore, determined by your earlier environmental influences.

Adler believed that people are absolute free agents with the will to determine their own personality via their own cognitive choices and reliance on their own innate creative selves. If you want to know who you truly are and why you are doing what you're doing, *in the now,* look *ahead,* and consciously move yourself forward toward what you have determined you want to be. When you focus on your future goals and ambitions, you align your personality with what it is you want to become and achieve. Freud, conversely, endorsed something called *efficient causality*—those experiences that push us forward from behind, making us what we are in the present.

"We do not have knowledge of a thing," purported Aristotle, "until we have grasped its why, that is to say, its cause."[2]

In stark contrast, Adler, much like Freud's early associate Karl Jung, advocated *final causality,* that which pulls us forward, from that which we determine lies ahead. The difference in causalities is the source: either influence from the past (of which we have no control) or influence from the future, or that which we create and ultimately control by our cognitive actions.

Adlerian philosophy observed that, on an innate level, human beings *feel inferior* and that these feelings of inferiority—or, better, a sense of feeling lost in an infinite world and universe—are the motivating force, the fire in the belly, the drive behind all personal striving for accomplishment and attainment of personal goals. In a sense, we start with absolutely nothing—perhaps even a deep insignificance in our own estimation—and we work our way up to what we *choose* to become, persistently building upon each successive failure and accomplishment. We *strive for excellence*—superiority, if you will—in order to compensate for the deeply innate feelings of inferiority. These are the things that push us to be better and to strive for being the very best we can be. This isn't about seeking superiority over others; it is about expressing and actualizing the drive toward perfecting ourselves. Eventually Adler expanded this idea of striving for the *ideal self* to striving to create a superior or perfect society to go along with it, and that our creative self is free to make up any sort of world it envisions and puts into implementation. This, however, was in contrast to German psychoanalyst Karen Horney, a contemporary of both Freud and Adler, who pushed her idea that humans don't strive for superiority; they strive for a self image built out of *idealism*. People don't believe their real self is acceptable, so, out of necessity and psychological survival, we create—out of whole cloth—an *idolized* self—the thing we think we *should* be.[3]

Do you see where this is going?

The entire notion of a race of Reptilians may be simply explained as a thing we've *devised from our own imaginations.* Just as we have devised religions built on spiritual experience and theory, we have done the very same thing with the notion of extraterrestrial races that live and operate behind the scenes of humanity. Just as with religion, there are things we call "evidences," yet no solid, empirical facts to back the claims, with the exception of historical studies and research that reveals a past history rife with nothing more than myth building within myth building within myth building. Simply go to your computer and type in the word "reptilians" (as I just did), and you will find more than 1,630,000 entries, and in the top 10 sites that appear in the list, half of them take you to something written by or based on the work of Zechariah Sitchin and David Icke, a self-proclaimed messiah, and the rest start off with phrases such as the following:

"Reptilians (also called reptoids, reptiloids, or draconians) are purported reptilian humanoids that play a prominent role in science fiction...."[4]

"Description: Typically, Reptilians are described as 6 to 8 feet tall, bipedal, having scaly green skin, have a bad odor, have large eyes usually yellow or gold with...."[5]

"The Reptilian Aliens which are called Reptoids are proportional in size to modern humans. They have a snake like or lizard appearance...."[6]

"I'm not claiming these people weren't 100% human at one time, what I am saying is that they invited the control and bodily takeover of Reptilians through blood...."[7]

"The teachings of the reptilian Ea, thereafter referred to as the esoteric mysticism of the snake brotherhood, caused a major shift in the perceptions of reality for...."[8]

"The Reptilians are the creation of the Carians, their parent race. They evolved on a planet...."[9]

"David Icke - The Reptilians - the Schism - Obama and the New World Order...Reptilian Experiencer and Author 'Susan Reed' Found Dead in the Bahamas...."[10]

"Alex Collier - On Reptilians - ETs and The Global Connection. - Alex Collier - On...Cosmic Explorers - Different Reptilian Factions on Earth. - Credo Mutwa On...."[11]

"Reptilian influence comes via Satanism which they created, and that controls Freemasonry (Phil Schneider found that the UN was run by tall grey aliens)...."[12]

At this point it may seem as if I am completely trashing and thrashing the Reptilian theory. In fact, I am doing nothing of the sort. In order to find what can withstand scrutiny and the boiling off of the dross, it is necessary to apply the "small s" skepticism of questioning everything—but not to point of offhandedly dismissing all. That's the job of "big S" Skeptics such as Michael Shermer, who sustains his income in much the same way as the paranormalists, ufologists, and weird-o-logians he decries. If you can't trust a researcher of the paranormal because they make money off of books, events, and TV, you certainly can't trust those who do the same thing on the other side of the philosophical fence, for the same reasons.

I have found that there are "small s" skeptics and "big S" Skeptics. I and many other like-minded philosophers are in the "small s" camp; we approach things with an open, yet questioning mind. We want to *know* the answers, but we do not do what the "big S" Skeptics do, and that is to dismiss questioning and make empirical statements such as "No it isn't"; "No it doesn't"; "You're completely wrong" without application of research, even if it's a fringe element. "Big S" Skepticism has (as has science, in many degrees), in proclaiming themselves better, more knowledgeable, or possessing of keener reason and more erudite insight, become the surrogate for religion, faith, and any train of thought outside what they deem as acceptable science or mainstream thinking. In a very real sense, Skepticism and science have established themselves as the "new religion," especially when they spend so much time decrying, and so little time researching the questions that fall outside established academia. The New Absolutism is that there are no absolutes.

Bringing this back to the psychological, it is clear that the human psyche is comprised of both the Freudian and Adlerian modes of primary expressions of the psyche: We humans have both the need to look to our pasts to determine where we came from, and the need to allow our future aspirations to pull us forward. Out of both, we create our present realities and live within the frameworks we compose for ourselves. Does this, then, bring to utter discredit the theory of alien interaction with human beings? Does it dismiss the completely the notion that there are races of extraterrestrial (ETs), interterrestrial (ITs), and ultraterrestrial (UTs) dwelling among us and influencing activity on this planet? Not necessarily. Just as I cannot dismiss the existence of God or the veracity of ancient religions on the simple notion that they are not quantifiable by the scientific method, I cannot dismiss the possibility that we have been visited by beings outside the realm of our sciences or understanding. This is where intelligent discussions on these matters collide as opposing, approaching trains on the same track.

"Oy!" you say, "Psychology! Religion! God! Mythology! When are you going to give us the aliens?" Hang on, folks; they're comin'.

The proofs and evidences that exist to substantiate a factual claim that a Reptilian race exists and operates on this planet are as evasive as the proofs and evidences required to prove the existence and work of God in humanity or the existence of ghosts of dead people materializing at midnight on the third full moon of every year. In short, there is no solid proof beyond personal experience and anecdotal evidence. Has that lack of measurable quantifiability prevented humanity from its historical, perpetual worship of God, gods, and other forms of divinities? Not in the least. As with religion, Reptilian/alien theory has its experiencers, such as the one mentioned in the opening of the introduction of this book, but they become the promulgators of personal, individual contact and intercourse (not limited to a sexual understanding) that have seen the unseen, spoken with the invisible, and learned the secret knowledges not known to others. These are the founders of "religious thought" in the alien field. I don't say this to cast any sort of negative light on their claims; I merely make the comparison to the spread of ancient religion and the evolution of religious thought within the alien culture. Just as Elil became Elohim, and Enki/Ea became Jehovah, so the progression of Reptilian esoterica has developed into its current state. The evangelists of the theory are as convinced in their perceptions and evidences as are the professors and theologians in different trains of religious thought, who many times are found to overlap the two fields. And why do they do that? Because the two fields are all one-in-same; they are outward expressions of inner desires—projections of what we want the world to be. That can be placed squarely on the shoulders of both religion and alienist trains of thinking in that they both hail to the spiritual make-up of the human psyche, those parts of the spiritual composition of individuals that need something to answer the greater questions of what lay beyond the explorable sciences.

Insert caveat here: Just because science and psychology seem to indicate that these things might not be so, does not qualify as the final answer on the topic. Remember: There exist some veils that we simply cannot pierce.

"Professing themselves to be wise, they became fools."
(Romans 1:22)

Where is the wise man? Where is the scholar? Where is the philosopher of this age? Has not God made foolish the wisdom of the world?
(1 Corinthians 1:20)

Everyone is senseless and without knowledge; every goldsmith is shamed by his idols. His images are a fraud; they have no breath in them.
(Jeremiah 10:14)

How can you say, "We are wise, for we have the law of the LORD," when actually the lying pen of the scribes has handled it falsely?
(Jeremiah 8:8)

My Reptile Can Kick Your Lizard's Ass

As we have seen, the archetypical serpent of ancient religion is certainly not the end of the story. The veneration of the snake in the ancient religious cultures of Sumer and Israel, China, Africa, and the ancient Americas is not where the influence of the serpent figure comes to a screeching halt. The presence of the serpent is not limited to the ancient religions of the world, though those religious/cultural mythologies are the philosophical foundations for ongoing reptilian mythologies. The psychology of needing or wanting something greater, built on human need for something to eliminate the foundational struggles of the past, has created some short coattails on which ride the current Reptilian and alien mythologies.

Author's rendition of the classic Reptilian. Image copyright of the author.

And perhaps this is the direct result of a humanity that wants something more than the traditional tales and entrenched religions. People are seeking for something more, so they create what they need and what they want to be. This, however, does not diminish the possibility that these notions have great efficacy, archaeologically, historically, cosmologically, and philosophically.

Our historical folklore is filled with imagery of the serpent reptile, ranging from science fiction and fantasy, to religious legends and modern conspiracy theories, ufology, and alien mythos to mysterious crypto-zoological beings. The Reptilians, as we have come to understand them in current-day mythology, can be found firmly ensconced in alien, otherworldly, and hollow earth lore as well as the theories of a race of intelligent, supernatural, inter-dimensional, highly developed reptile-like humanoids. They have become the stuffs of cult fiction, pseudoscientific theories, and the topics of the writings of New Age conspiracists.

David Icke, Riley Martin, and John Rhodes, stand out among the most recognizable claimants promoting the Reptilian existence and conspiracies, and though there are similarities to their versions of these beings, they also represent vastly differing theories as to their origins and interactions with the planet earth and the human race. None of them is anything less than malevolent. Martin's book, *The Coming of Tan,* is a memoir of his experiences as a sharecropper's kid who was taken on board an alien spacecraft. In his book he claims to have a personal knowledge of a race of Reptilians known as the Targzissians, an evil race of Reptilians who manage to coexist with six other types of aliens on a mother ship near Saturn.

On his tumblr.com profile, Rhodes says of his himself and his work: "My name is John Rhodes and I am a researcher, explorer and lecturer in the realms of ufology, occulted archaeology and metaphysics. In this report, I will be providing you with compelling evidence, gathered over many years of research, as to our genealogical connections with the overlord reptilian alien race and the occulted historical archaeology that clearly demonstrates that these reptilian beings have coexisted on this planet Earth with us for thousands of years prior to our current era."[13]

David Icke speaks of good and bad Reptilians fighting it out for domination of the Earth while clothed in cloned human skin, mostly infiltrating the royal families of Europe. (We will focus a bit on Icke in Chapter 7.)

Reptoids is a descriptive manufactured word defining Reptilian-Humanoid beings. It is the most culturally popular name used to describe these extraterrestrial beings, although they are also referenced as dinosauroids,[14] or lizardfolk or lizardmen (both *Dungeons and Dragons* terms, for you gamers out there). Other names include Draconians,[15] which draw their name from the many proponents of the Draconian constellation as the point of origin for these otherworldly visitors, as well as Saurians and the hypothetical Dinoauroids.[16] Although you may seek out other source points, they are generally found referenced by name in the plethora of Internet sites that neither state source material nor point of origin, yet are found repeated over and over again into the countless hundreds of thousands. In these accountings the Reptilians are often described as having soft, scaley skin that is green or golden-brown in color. Yet, despite their similarity to Reptilian archetypes throughout mythology, no one has produced even a modicum of proof of the existence of Reptilian-Humanoids, and allegations of their existence can at best be referred to as crypto-zoological or pseudoscientific as opposed to a recorded genus or species.

Dale Russell, a Canadian-born geologist and paleontologist, was the first to purport an extraterrestrial theory as to the extinction of the dinosaurs in the form of an asteroid collision or supernova.[17] He is also invented what became the highly controversial "Dinosauroid Thought

Experiment," a process that incorporates the employing of imaginary situations to help us understand the way things really are, or in other words, a hypothetical imagining of what could be if certain criteria had happened. This thought experiment resulted in his highly controversial, previosuly mentioned Dinosauroid.

Reptilians and the claims to their existence are nothing new. They are not simply the product of the mid-20th-century ufological explosion, nor are they a science fiction invention of Hollywood, however well-capitalized they might be in that market, with movies such as *The Alligator People* (1959), *Enemy Mine* (1985), *Conan the Barbarian* (1982), *Krull* (1983), *V—the Miniseries* (1984), the *Star Trek* franchise, and the list goes on. Experiencers, contactees, and abductees have, for centuries, made claims that they have been in contact with Reptilian peoples, yet there still exists no substantive proof beyond the stuffs of anecdotal evidences and personal experience as to just who the Reptilians are and where they actually come from, if indeed they exist as a race at all. Arguments have been made that Reptilians are Earth-evolved beings that expanded out into the cosmos long ago, and others will conversely argue that they came here from the aptly named constellation of Draco, hence the "Draconian" moniker.

According to proponents of the Reptilian theory, there has been enough information derived from the many contactee and experiencer reports and stories as to build a formidable trove of information about these beings. As a result, the Reptilian conspiracy *believers* emphatically insist they are in a position to *deliver the truth* behind the origins of the Reptilian aliens, revealing precisely who these beings are and exactly what is behind their hidden agenda. Those unwilling to listen and heed the warnings will be doomed to fall under the influence and enslavement of the Reptilians.

After researching copious amounts of information on the origins of these Draconian Reptilians, I was able to boil down the varying stories, hypotheses, and myriad personal accounts into an acceptable amalgam that bears all the elements of the following:

The Reptilians evolved on two separate planets, one being Earth and the other a planet near Draconis, the brightest star in the aptly named serpentine-shaped constellation of Draco (Latin for "Dragon"). "Draco" is circumpolar—that is, never setting—for many observers in the northern hemisphere's night sky. It was one of the 48 constellations listed by second-century astronomer Ptolemy and remains one of the 88 modern constellations today. From these two vastly distant planets of origin, two distinctly different races of Reptilian would evolve and help shape our planet and civilization as we know it today.

As the two Reptilian races evolved, it was known to the Draconian Reptilians, an evil spirited, warrior species, manipulative and deceitful in nature, that the Earthly Reptoids were a peaceful, good-hearted race. The Draconians were so evolved that, like the Arcturians, they surpassed the physical limitations of their material bodies, eschewing—despite their evil nature—their carnivorous need to eat and digest solid foods, developing the ability to ingest their nutrients through pure energy alone. The only problem was that their required energy food source was bad, evil energy. Accordingly, in order to survive, the Draconians must ingest pure evil energy, and it is this fact alone that turns simple self-preservation for the Draconians into an evil agenda.

In order to survive, the Draconian Reptilians are also rumored to have created the race that we have come to know as the Alien Greys as their slave race cloned as a source for nutrition. As the Draconian civilization continued to grow and expand, however, there was wrench in the gears, for as the Reptilians grew in numbers, so did their slave race of Greys. Soon the Greys, weary of being drained of their negative energy by the evil race of overlords, revolted, resulting in their freedom from the consumptive bondage of their creators, the Draconian Reptilians. They left their captors and, apparently, continued on with their own agenda.

But now, bereft of their evil-energied clone slave race, the Draconians desperately needed new sources of nutrition. So they set out in their mighty but evil fleet of starships, seeking other planets that had populations on which they could feed. But, of course, the energy of those populations had to be comprised of bad and evil energy, so the search for the right planet was painstaking and long. One can only assume the cannibalism that must've taken place during those long generations of space travel, furtively seeking a source of food.

One day, the fleet was all abuzz, for a new source of energy consumption had been located! The Draconians had stumbled across the planet Earth. Their discovery of Earth is difficult to reconcile with the fact that they seemed, by various accounts, to already know that the Reptoids of Earth were benevolent and good-spirited, and that represents one of the many gaping cracks in the narrative. As the story goes, it was here they observed the highly advanced, yet peaceful race of Reptilian-like aliens known as Reptoids. But far more important to the Draconians were the human beings indigenous to Earth. They set a plan in motion to utilize the human population on Earth as the source for their evil energy nutrition. They first needed to eliminate and remove the

Earth-evolved Reptoids in order to launch their Reptilian Agenda and manipulate a race of evil-minded humans for their energy consumption.

At this point, there are gaps in the storyline, but after successfully forcing most of the Reptoids to leave the Earth, Draconian Reptilians began to work their way into and influence the civilizations of Earth's ancient past. Rumored reports state that some Earth-evolved Reptoids still exist beneath the streets and farms of our planet, and within the subterranean caverns of the Earth, secretly operating as freedom fighters for the human population of Earth, countering the Draconian Reptilian Alien agenda.

Today, power struggles among the Alien forces have thwarted an outright invasion of our planet. Reptilian Aliens from the Draco Constellation still have a fixed eye on our planet and have emissaries here on Earth performing the vital tasks to ensure that humans remain on the track of corruption, hatred, and ego-centric goals. The more evil, the more food.

Now, pull this leg and it plays "Jingle Bells."

I honestly did not know, after reading several sources on the Draconian story, whether to laugh uncontrollably or simply shake my head slowly from side to side. And you thought the story of the Garden of Eden seemed implausible.

After dissecting the various stories and myriad accounts of the so-called Reptilian Agenda, the preceding story was what emerged. Granted, some of the versions I encountered were meticulously well-written, providing "research notes" (mostly citing Sitchin, Icke, and others) and eloquent narrative. Others read like a fifth-grade essay project, but for the most part, they all said, pretty much, the same thing—reading like the script to a poorly conceived, made-for-television, B-grade science-fiction thriller with even poorer CGI. If you want a weekend's worth of good entertainment, simply conduct an Internet search on the "Reptilians," then start reading the various versions of where they came from, how they got here, and what they're up to. Then note, as you read, the absolute lack of source material and references, and you become as frustrated as I was attempting to locate any accounts that bore even a modicum of presented fact beyond the individual author's *feelings* and ungrounded, unsubstantiated storytelling (and in most cases, not even good storytelling).

In short, if these accounts were all we had to go on, I would think it would be pretty easy to chalk this all up to overactive imaginations and erstwhile yet sloppy interpretations of personal experiences set against an even looser grasp of history and the anthropology of myth.

Hitting Below Orion's Belt

"There are good reasons to assume the man does not experience his fellowman as a member of the same species.... For him different language, customs, dress and other criteria perceived by the mind rather than by instincts determine who is a co-specific and who is not, and any group which is slightly different is not supposed to share in the same humanity... precisely because he lacks instinctive equipment, also lacks the experience of the identity of his species and experiences the stranger as if he belonged to another species; in other words, it's man's humanity that makes him so inhuman."

—Erich Fromm

The fact that there are so many stories and theories attempting to establish the existence of extraterrestrial and intraterrestrial Reptilians on this planet speaks to one of two things:

1. Extraterrestrial Reptilians actually exist and interact with humanity based on the over-abundance of stories and experiencer accounts.

2. The over-abundance of stories provides a distinct picture of how "believers" in certain phenomena attempt to establish their case, while presenting absolutely no quantifiable evidence, thus contributing to an ever-increasing cache of unsubstantiated stories and information.

In other words, there's a lot of information out there that is the product of over-worked imaginations based on the supposed scholarly presentations of a very small handful of researchers.

It's like the existence of God and the hundreds of religions that have sprouted from that one particular idea: Everyone starts with the root concept and either mimics what has been taught, or builds their own offshoot denomination or religion. In recent years I have read more accounts of the Reptilians on the Internet that are precise, repetitive, word-for-word copies of theories presented by Zechariah Sitchin, David Icke, and others of like-mind, whom I would refer to as founders of the contemporary thinking on the Reptilian Theory, that I believe there are very few original thoughts or unique research out there. Most of these accounts are presented without any reference to their source material, nor any evidences or proofs establishing their cases, but contain the very same language, parroting the information presented by one or two major proponents.

Despite believing that there is something that has interfered with and interrupted the bloodlines of humanity, I tend toward the latter, above, in that there seems to be an awful lot of scrambling to make a story fit the preconceived notion, as opposed to empirical data to substantiate the claim. And there exists a completely different take on the entire notion of extraterrestrial life making contact with the human race. The astro-biologists and exo-biologists who study life as it may or may not exist on other planets have a daunting task at their fingertips. Though we have not even mastered the intricacies of human life and other forms of life on *this* planet, the study of places billions of light years from where we exist is theoretical at best, impossible at worst, yet we still engage in the study and research, all because we want to have some idea of what is out there—and speculate on whether or not *what is out there* may know anything about *us.* On top of that, to even suggest that there might be life out there that is similar if not more advanced than life on Earth is still met with general ridicule and eye-rolling scoffs. To some who criticize, the notion flies in the face of reason and/or religion. To others, it is simply an irrelevancy that when stacked against the tumultuous intricacies of life on this planet, let alone within local governments, politics, poverty, war, communities, and even families, is completely without meaning. If we can't figure things out *here,* then how are we supposed to try to connect with something that exists in a place beyond the stars, so out-of-context and out-of-reach to us humans? "If they exist, why don't they just fly their little starship space saucers over and say 'Hi!'?" is the arrogant response, and "If they had that technology, why would they want to come *here?*" is the answer for those who believe that our understanding of science is the unit by which we measure the dimensions of the greater galaxy and universe. Perhaps, for extraterrestrial life, contact with our species is as risky to them as Fromm suggests in the quote here, defined by humanity's intolerance to his fellow man.

I am as dichotomous on the subject of extraterrestrial contact as I am on the idea of God. To evangelicals, I am a heretic and a reprobate—a back-slidden blasphemer who has abandoned the true faith. To the atheist, I am a Bible-thumping, Word-of-God preaching, Christian apologist. And that is because I am decisively middle of the road in that I accept the unprovable possibility that there is a God, but I have deeply rooted questions and doubts, and seek better answers than the regurgitated pap offered up in most churches.

I have the very same dichotomous approach when it comes to my stance on ancient alien theory and the existence of Reptilians and Greys: I want to see the evidence that doesn't force my hand to squeeze the square peg into the round hole. Yet, based on my multicultural religious studies, I have very little doubt that this planet has been visited by non-human intelligences. Call them gods, devils, angels, demons, or extraterrestrials, it's not even a stretch for me to believe that in the vastness of the outward moving, ever-expanding universe there are not races intelligent and advanced enough to have come to this place and possibly even still live here, as colloquial and local as that may seem. After all, ancient myth combined with historical documentation, film footage, experiencer and abduction cases, leaked government information, and numerous other data speak loudly to their existence. The bigger questions for me, as with many who have come before me, are: "Who are the main players?"; "How do we fit into the scheme?"; "After we know these things, where will that take us?"

The entire history of the alien mythos repeatedly asserts the existence of many different types of alien beings present on this planet today. Anecdotally speaking, even I am only one step removed from a dear, old friend who encountered and became intimately involved with a mysterious man who reported that he worked for a facility in New Mexico that sank dozens of stories under the ground, headquartering several dozens of alien species that live and interact on this planet. According to this shadowy character, these alien races have been restricted from any interference with human beings or their affairs, at least in the greater sense. But if this is true, why are we seeing an ever-increasingly number of experiencers and abductees repeatedly describing only two distinct types of intelligent life forms with whom they've interacted (the Greys and the Reptilians)? And why is it that *they* seem to have exclusive rights of interference with humans? If interaction between these beings and our own species has been occurring throughout history, as legend and myth could seem to indicate, then where is the substantive evidence as to their existence? Where are they from, and what is their business with, or interest in, us?

I am firmly convinced that the contact we have experienced with non-human entities is inextricably linked to the mythologies of the ancients and that the contact we may be experiencing today has not only a metaphysical connection to the past, but a physical one as well.

The legacy of the ancient serpent has become the modern history of the Reptilian connection. Is there any substantive reality to it, or is it all simply the extrapolation of ancient mythology into the current age, all driven by the *need* to have something more?

The Serpent's Bloodline

P
A
R
T

III

Chapter Five

The Remnant of the Nephilim

¹When mankind began to multiply on the earth and daughters
were born to them, ²the sons of God saw that the daughters
of mankind were beautiful, and they took any they chose as
wives for themselves. ³And the Lord said, "My Spirit will not
remain with mankind forever, because they are corrupt. Their
days will be 120 years." ⁴The Nephilim were on the earth both
in those days and afterward, when the sons of God came to the
daughters of mankind, who bore children to them. They were
the powerful men of old, the famous men.
(Genesis 6:1–4)

It's a very familiar story to you by now. The Elohim came to the earth,
according to the Old Testament's Book of Genesis and the apocryphal
book of Enoch, and intermingled with humans. They chose women,
cohabited with them, married them, impregnated them, and produced
offspring: the hybrid race of Nephilim, the children of those Elohim
who had left their place and come down. Prior to those events, one
of the Elohim, forever known as the Serpent character, Nachash, had
an intimate encounter with Eve in the Garden of Eden, revealing forbidden knowledge and impregnating her with his seed, producing the
very first of the human-Elohim crossbred Nephilim, Cain. According
to the religions wrapped around the events of the Book of Genesis, the

consequence of this activity was the fall of humanity from the grace of God, spiritually ushering in the need for a system of blood redemption and a savior who would be their Messiah—the kinsman redeemer. The God of the Hebrews cursed the Elohim, Nachash, prophesying perpetual conflict between his offspring and the offspring of the human woman, Eve, who was the mother of all humanity. What followed in the biblical record were lengthy cataloguings of the descendents of Adam—which, we have noted, did not include Eve's firstborn twin son, Cain, as he was the child of Nachash of the Elohim. This genealogical record was set in place to establish the "pure" human bloodline from which the kinsman redeemer was to come. What is glaringly left out of the biblical account-ing, though, is the line of Nachash. We read that Cain was banished from Eden after murdering his younger twin brother, Abel. Exiled from Eden, Cain left behind the only two other people mentioned in the Bible as being on the earth at that time: Adam and Eve. He went out into a world void of inhabitants and civilization, east to the Land of Nod. Once there, the passage tells us that he made love to his wife (of course—what else would you do after being banished from the only place on earth?), whom he either brought with him from Eden—meaning she was one of his sisters not named in the account of the first family—or a woman he met in his wanderings. She, in turn, bore him a son, whom Cain named Enoch.

And there in the Land of Nod, Cain built a city, most likely a wooden enclosure around a few huts, in honor of his new son, and named the city after him, Enoch. Of the subsequent history of this little city we know very little, but of the name of the city we know a very great deal. Without entering into too much detail regarding changes in pronun-ciation that occur in the course of the development of a language, it seems necessary to point out here that the sound represented by the letter N is often reproduced as an R. The CH sound that terminates the name *Enoch* may be replaced by a K or G, or a GH sound. These sorts of linguistic changes are very common in ancient tongues, and in relation to biblical city mounds, or tells, the people living around these cites kept the name places fairly intact throughout the passage of millennia. This revealed a very important city in antiquity that appeared under the name *Uruk,* and a study of cuneiform soon revealed that this could equally well be pronounced *Unuk,* which was recognized as identical with the biblical word *Enoch.*[1]

What is more interesting is that the name Uruk/Unuk became synonymous with the word *city,* and not simply a mere city, but a city of great historical importance. The word in its raw form actually means, "the First City."

Nod [נוד] is the Hebrew root of the verb "to wander" [לנדוד] and is obviously an etymological causation intended to explain the wandering, nomadic lifestyle of Cain and his future putative descendants, the Kenites. This sort of play on words is typical of rabbinic writings and suggests that this is a later scribal interpretation, which was more than likely inserted to suggest that Cain's descendants were without territory—in other words, nomadic. Additionally, the Hebrew language did not exist prior to the time of Abraham, who lived some 4,000 years after the time of Cain. The language Cain and his descendents would have spoken was probably a Nilotic/Kushitic language closer to Old Arabic (Dedanite). So, although Cain built the first city, his descendents were forever known as wanderers, those without home, territory, or place to exist. And these were the offspring of Nachash.

It is interesting to note that, though the Nephilim mentioned in Genesis 6 are offspring of the Sons of God, the bene ha 'Elohim, they are not the children of the serpent. Nachash was not their father. So the Nephilim of Genesis 6 are not the "serpent seed," though it is quite possible that the descendents of Cain had grown large enough to be

The Secret History of the Reptilians

part of the hybrid race of Nephilim that had encompassed all of the known earth, corrupting the bloodlines of humanity up until the time of Noah. There is no direct information on this point of detail, though it can be extrapolated from the rest of the information that this is probably so.

The Serpent Seed Doctrine

So many times and in so many ways, current Christianity operates under presumptions that the text from which they pull their doctrine has been accurately translated, or presents a factual accounting of what they think they are understanding. Never is this truer than when fundamental Christianity takes dogmatic stances on the person and character of Lucifer/Satan/the devil, as well as the passages used to substantiate his presence in the Bible and in important doctrine-establishing passages of scripture. The lack of careful examination of the biblical text about the Serpent Seed Doctrine reveals a complete misunderstanding of the figure of Satan. The biblical passages that are forced to support the theory that Satan is a fallen angel is a tragic theological conundrum in the churches of modern Christianity, because the result is a complete misunderstanding of several applied biblical passages, the result of which has created a corrupt doctrine that perpetuates a complete error about the creature known as Satan.

When YHWH (Yahweh/Jehovah), the Mighty-One, revealed Himself to Moses and had Moses write the Hebrew Torah (also known as the Pentateuch, the first five books of the Bible), there was not one single mention of an evil angel named Satan, or a plurality of evil angels—or, for that matter, *any* being that could tempt you in your mind to transgress the law of God. In fact the main point of the Torah is to proclaim that there is only one Mighty-One, and that one Mighty-One is YHWH (Yahweh/Jehovah). In Exodus 20:2–3 we find these words:

² "I am YHWH (Yahweh) your Mighty-One, which has brought you out of the land of Egypt, out of the house of bondage. ³ You shall have no other mighty one before Me."

Deuteronomy 4:35–36 says:

³⁵ Unto you it was shown, that you might know that YHWH (Yahweh), ³⁶ He is the Almighty, there is none else beside Him. Know therefore this day, and consider it in your mind, that YHWH (Yahweh/Jehovah) He is the Almighty in heaven above and upon earth beneath: there is none else" (author's emphasis).

The first point to understanding this Serpent Seed Doctrine, is to understand that it is generally looked down upon as an heretical doctrine by those who claim to have the truth of God's Word" on their side. Before we say a single word about the doctrine itself, it is important to note that we are looking at it from a "religion-spin-free zone"—from a point of view that sees such statements as "Let's look at this from the perspective of one and only true word of God" as being thickly entrenched in religion-making and religion-keeping, as opposed to fact-finding.

If you wonder what the Serpent Seed Doctrine is, well, you actually already know, if you have read this book up to this point. The Serpent Seed, Dual Seed, or Two-Seedline is a controversial doctrine according to which the Serpent in the Garden of Eden mated with Eve, and the offspring of their sexual union was Cain, thereby bequeathing a bloodline that threads throughout humanity. Bingo. There it is.

The reaction in fundamentalist Christian circles is *What!? Eve mated with Satan and bore the devil's child?! And there is a line of descendency? Impossible. Not in my Bible!* But you have to disavow yourself of contemporary notions and fictions such as the idea behind *Rosemary's Baby* or such other works when attempting to understand these concepts. **Nachash was not Satan. He was not the devil.** He may not have even been Lucifer, despite the later works in the Bible attributing Lucifer/

Satan/the devil to the Serpent in the Garden. And keep in the forefront of your mind, the only biblical passages making this claim do not spell it out in precise detail, nor can they, generally, withstand the scrutiny of criticism on a linguistic level. *Never* is Nachash, the Serpent in Genesis, directly said to be Lucifer, Satan, or the devil.

Here are the few references in the Bible that some theologians use to establish that the Serpent in the Garden has anything to with Lucifer, Satan, or the devil. See what you think.

Ezekiel 28:11–19

Ezekiel 28:11–19 is considered to be the first extrapolated reference to Lucifer/Satan/the devil as being present in the Garden of Eden. It was written approximately 1,000 years *after* the writing of the Book of Genesis. It is a lament written for the fallen King of Tyre, and the Christian church has rendered its meaning to stand as a metaphor for Lucifer/Satan/the devil. In actuality, it is not about Lucifer/Satan/the devil at all. Here is how the authorized version of the biblical passage reads:

Lamentation for the King of Tyre
(author's emphasis throughout)

[11]Moreover the word of the Lord came to me, saying, [12]"Son of man, take up a lamentation for the *King of Tyre,* and say to him, 'Thus says the Lord God:
"You were the seal of perfection,
Full of wisdom and perfect in beauty.

[13]*You were in Eden, the garden of God;*
Every precious stone was your covering:
The sardius, topaz, and diamond,
Beryl, onyx, and jasper,
Sapphire, turquoise, and emerald with gold.
The workmanship of your timbrels and pipes
Was prepared for you on the day you were created.

14"*You were the anointed cherub* who covers;
I established you;
You were on the holy mountain of God;
You walked back and forth in the midst of fiery stones.

15You were perfect in your ways from the day you were created,
Till iniquity was found in you.

16"By the abundance of your trading
You became filled with violence within,
And you sinned;
Therefore I cast you as a profane thing
Out of the mountain of God;
And I destroyed you, O covering cherub,
From the midst of the fiery stones.

17"Your heart was lifted up because of your beauty;
You corrupted your wisdom for the sake of your splendor;
I cast you to the ground,
I laid you before kings,
That they might gaze at you.

18"You defiled your sanctuaries
By the multitude of your iniquities,
By the iniquity of you trading;
Therefore I brought fire from your midst;
It devoured you,
And I turned you to ashes upon the earth
In the sight of all who saw you.

19All who knew you among the peoples are astonished at you;
You have become a horror,
And shall be no more forever."

However, there are many translation issues with the preceding verses, which render it to read as a figurative descriptive metaphor for Lucifer/Satan/the devil. On examination, it says nothing of the sort. Here is how the passage is rendered in the Hebrew language in which it was originally written. Compare it to the rendering of the passage above (again, author's emphasis throughout):

11–12And the word of YHWH (Yahweh) came to me saying, 'Son of man, raise a dirge over the king of Tyre. Say to him, "The Master YHWH (Yahweh) says this: You were once a *seal-print [exemplar] of perfection*, full of wisdom, perfect in beauty. 13You *came into luxury, a paradise from Elohim,* gems of every kind were your covering, Sardin, topaz, diamond, chrysolite, onyx, jasper, sapphire, carbuncle, emerald. Your jingling beads were of gold, and the spangles you wore were made for you on the day of your birth. 14I had *provided you with a guardian cherub*; you were in the set-apart mountain of Elohim, and you walked proudly among the stones that flashed with fire. 15You were blameless in all your ways from the day of your birth until iniquity came to light. 16Your busy trading has filled you with lawlessness and sin, so I thrust you down from the mountain of Elohim, and *the guardian cherub banished [or destroyed] you* from among the stones that flashed like fire. 17Your heart has made you arrogant because of your beauty. You have corrupted your wisdom because of your splendor. *I have thrown you to the ground; I have made you a spectacle for other kings.* 18So great was your sin in your wicked trading, that you have desecrated your sanctuaries. So I kindled a fire within you, to consume you. I left you as ashes on the ground for all to see. 19Of the nations, all who know you were aghast; you became waste, gone forever.'"

The major textual problems with the previous passage require a highly technical linguistic research, bringing in many intricate details from not only the Hebrew language, but also the LXX (the Septuagint, or Greek translation of the Old Testament). So rather than write 10 pages of textual criticism, linguistics, and translation issues, let me simply state that the comparatives made between the King of Tyre and Lucifer/Satan/the devil are insufficient translations, and one needs to go back to the Hebrew and Septuagint to understand the proper translation as rendered in the second version of the passage above.[2,3]

Job 38:7

Job 38:7 is also used to speak of the Serpent being Lucifer:

"When the morning stars sang together, And all the sons of God shouted for joy?"

Because Lucifer/Satan was a created being, and because Eden was guarded by cherubim after the Fall, some scholars say that Lucifer/Satan must have been in Eden between his creation and the fall of humanity. Many scholars believe, based on Job 38:7, that all the angels, including Lucifer, were created on or before Day Four of creation week along with the sun, moon, and stars, only two days before the creation of Adam and Eve. But remember: Lucifer was a member of the Divine Council, one of the Elohim, the "Sons of God." Though Lucifer may have been the Serpent, this verse says absolutely nothing about him being so. This verse also establishes for me that the "days" of Genesis were more than likely not 24-hour, solar days, but probably epochs of time. If they were literal 24-hour, solar days, then Lucifer decided he would take over God's throne, rebelled, and fell from grace in roughly four to seven days from his moment of creation. (That's another topic that we could trail off into for many pages.)

2 Corinthians 11:3

2 Corinthaisn 11:3 mentions the Serpent in the Garden, but make no connection to Lucifer/Satan. The following is a comparative statement, not an identifying one.

But I fear, lest somehow, as the serpent deceived Eve by his craftiness, so your minds may be corrupted from the simplicity that is in Christ.

Book of Revelation

The following three passages are taken from the writings of the Apostle John, who in his old age was imprisoned for the faith on the Isle of Patmos. While there, he had extraordinary prophetic visions that he recorded in what is known to be, chronologically, the last book written in the Bible's New Testament, the Book of Revelation. Here are the three references he makes to Satan, whom he calls the "great dragon." They are not presented in their full context here, but they are fairly stand-alone in their reference. They were written nearly 1,500 years after the Book of Genesis.

Revelation 12:9

> So *the great dragon* was cast out, *that serpent of old, called the Devil and Satan,* who deceives the whole world; he was cast to the earth, and his angels were cast out with him (author's emphasis).

Revelation 12:13–17

> 13Now when the *dragon* (author's emphasis) saw that he had been cast to the earth, he persecuted the woman who gave birth to the male Child. 14But the woman was given two wings of a great eagle, that she might fly into the wilderness to her place, where she is nourished for a time and times and half a time, from the presence of the serpent. 15So the serpent spewed water out of his mouth like a flood after the woman, that he might cause her to be carried away by the flood. 16But the earth helped the woman, and the earth opened its mouth and swallowed up the flood which the dragon had spewed out of his mouth. 17And the dragon was enraged with the woman, and he went to make war with the rest of her offspring, who keep the commandments of God and have the testimony of Jesus Christ.

Revelation 20:2

> He laid hold of the dragon, that serpent of old, who is the Devil and Satan, and bound him for a thousand years...

1 Peter 5:8

1 Peter 5:8, in one final biblical passage, renders the metaphoric Satan in a completely different form than the Serpent, as found in Eden.

Be alert and of sober mind. Your enemy the *devil prowls around like a roaring lion* (author's emphasis) looking for someone to devour.

So what was the purpose of this little foray into the Serpent Seed Doctrine? It was to establish that the doctrine is not heretical to church teachings, for it simply does not refer to Satan as the entity of the Genesis passages. More than anything, it establishes that the Serpent in the Garden of Eden was completely unique from the biblical references to Lucifer, Satan, or the devil—and even those references are obscure in Hebrew, extrapolated and forced into meaning by the teachings of the Christian church.

The Serpent Seed Doctrine should rightfully have the word *Doctrine* removed from the title, for it is nothing more than a statement of fact as substantiated within the textual passage where we find the interaction between the Serpent, Nachash, and Eve, the wife of Adam. Moreover, the Reptilian race that interacts with humanity is beginning to look more and more as if it is less a host of alien invaders, but rather a linkage, both physically and metaphysically, to the bloodline of the Serpent.

The doctrinal belief of the Serpent Seed is still held by some adherents of Christian Identity, a label applied to a wide variety of loosely affiliated believers and churches with a white supremacist theology. Most promote a racist interpretation of Christianity, claiming that the Jews, as descendants of Cain, are also descended from the Serpent. This is a belief that has surface throughout history and was adhered to by none other than one Adolf Hitler.

Chapter Six

The Merovingian Connection

I f you believe there is a lot of mythology and mystery surrounding the Serpent and the Elohim, be prepared to pull up your iron shorts and pull on your thinking cap, because the Merovingian connection to the Serpent and the Elohim will quite possibly blow your mind. If you have heard the term *Merovingian(s)* used, you may have heard them referenced in connection to the Holy Grail and the search for that sacred cup in the Arthurian legends, and still have absolutely no idea who or what they are—and that they have been tied into the mythology of the Serpent. You will now find an astonishing connection to all the mythologies presented thus far in both *The Rise and Fall of the Nephilim* and everything in this book thus far. But, as always, let's start at the beginning.

In the Dark Ages

Ready for a little history lesson? For roughly 300 years between the fifth and eighth centuries, the Merovingians (sometimes referred to by their contemporaries as the "long-haired kings," as they wore their hair long in ostentatious comparison to the closer-cropped hairstyles of the rest of the Franks) were a Salian Frankish dynasty that came into power, ruling the region known as Francia, largely synonymous with ancient Gaul, inclusive of modern-day France, as the regional name implies. From the third century on, the Salian Franks appear in the historical

157

records as warlike Germanic barbarians and pirates, bitter ancestral enemies of the Gaulic Celts, and avowed allies of the Romans known as *Laeti*, a word used by the Romans to denote the barbarian tribes (literally "babblers" of out-land tongues; that is, foreigners, people from outside the Empire) who gave them fealty, serving as underlord serfs who swore allegiance and provided soldiers for the Roman armies, resulting in a rag-tag alliance with Rome. This granted them the right to be the first Germanic tribe settling permanently on Roman land. In 358, they entered into political agreement with the Romans and moved into the region known as Toxandria, which comprises roughly the area of current-day Holland and Belgium.[1]

By the seventh century, the Salians fully adopted Frankish identity and gradually dropped their identification with Salian roots and heritage altogether. It's interesting to note that the Merovingian kings operated under a rather socialistic system of governance, as defined by current-day standards. The king redistributed conquered wealth and real estate among his followers, and this was not just given to the nobility, as it apparently extended to the indentured peasantry. Some scholars have attributed this to the Merovingians as lacking a manageable understanding of public affairs, but there is also the view that they knew precisely what they were doing, and this was an act meant to foster loyalty among their people.

It was the son of Meroveus/Merovic (the ruler from whom the name Merovingian is derived), the leader of the Salian Franks, Childeric I (c. 457–481), who founded the Merovingian dynasty. His son Clovis I (481–511), however, was the man who united the Gaulic tribes and territories under Merovingian rule. After his death the Merovingian family seemed to be in a constant state of in-fighting and back-and-forth skirmishes for power, but when threatened by outsiders, the Merovingians always presented a unified front, standing together with unified purpose and intent. They were the ultimate power in the region. During the final century of Merovingian rule, the dynasty was increasingly pushed into a more or less ceremonial role. In 752, Pope Zachary formally deposed the last ruler of the Merovingian dynasty, Childeric III, bringing to an end the Merovingian era.[2,3]

Christianity eventually started to take a foothold with the Merovingians, at least in the sense of being "Christianized." An Irish monk named Columbanus, who was eventually elevated to sainthood by the Church, enjoyed great influence due to his sincere friendship with Queen Balthid, the wife of Clovis II. The Merovingians established numerous monasteries throughout their empire and awarded them to their loyal lords who funded the abbeys and monasteries, granting them bishoprics and titles as abbots. Many of them, due to their financial support, were even granted sainthoods.

Before we go further with the Merovingians, let's take an intermediate trip, wading through the theories behind the bloodline of Jesus Christ, which will intersect us with the Merovingians once more.

Mr. and Mrs. Jesus Christ

There is an enduring, shadowy, hypothetical mythology surrounding the ancestry and lineage of Jesus Christ, with the trail originating in first-century Palestine, leading to the thrones of the Merovingian kings of Franco Europe. It has been claimed that Mary Magdalene was Jesus' concubine, and Mormonism claims that Jesus was a polygamist. There are also theories that Jesus turned, of all things, atheist, married Mary, and went to Europe. If any genuine historical data to back any of these claims existed, they have been lost to antiquity. What we have today are countless books on the subject, some rich in history, and others just as rich in conspiratorial magma and speculative kookiness. So, it is left to the interpretations of the readers of the many literary works glutting the shelves—both fiction and non-fiction—to determine their veracity, in lieu of any solid proof.

In the highly intriguing, yet equally controversial book *The Holy Blood and the Holy Grail* (1982), the Merovingians are presented as kings who established their power by claiming they were descended from the bloodline of Jesus Christ, who, if the claim were true, would had to have been married and producing offspring in order to leave a traceable bloodline.[4] This book, as one might imagine, caused an immense stir around the world, and the ideas contained in the book were deemed blasphemous enough for it to be banned in some Roman Catholic-dominated countries. Response from the historical and academic fields was quite negative, and critics of the book tore it to shreds, claiming that the bulk of the claims, ancient mysteries, and conspiracy theories presented as fact were nothing short of pseudo-historical. Famed book critic Anthony Burgess wrote of the book, "It is typical of my unregenerable soul that I can only see this as a marvelous theme for a novel."[5] Dan Brown did just that and utilized the theme for his international best-selling 2003 novel, *The DaVinci Code.*

Despite the criticisms, and even the authors of the book making statements that some elements had to be fictionalized in order to fill the untraceable gaps in an invisible lineage of Jesus, the book presented enough historical fact as to prompt many historians—off the beaten path of convention and peer review—to dig a little deeper, giving us the Jesus bloodline that linked into the Merovingians.

As might be imagined, *The Holy Blood and the Holy Grail* spawned innumerable other books and documentaries exploiting both the veracity of the claims and the criticisms made in the book. In his 1996 book, *Bloodline of the Holy Grail: The Hidden Lineage of Jesus Revealed,* Sir Laurence Gardner picks up the gauntlet and presents what he said were actual pedigree charts of the lineage of Jesus of Nazareth and Mary Magdalene. Gardiner maintained that these family trees proved beyond all doubt that the biblical couple were the ancestors of all royal European families,[6] claiming that this, indeed, linked them to the contemporary

Reptilian conspiracy theories that state all modern European Royal families are alien Reptilians, operating under the influence of a hidden race of extraterrestrials bent on the destruction of humanity. In his 2000 sequel, *Genesis of the Grail Kings: The Explosive Story of Genetic Cloning and the Ancient Bloodline of Jesus,* Gardiner makes extraordinary claims that there is physical evidence—outside the biblical genealogies—that the bloodline of Jesus of Nazareth could be traced back to Adam and Eve. If you are Christian, this is already something that can be established in biblical texts, as the followers of Jesus set out to establish the blood tie between Jesus, Mary, and Joseph to the royal house of King David, then all the way back to Noah and then to Seth, the third son of Adam. Gardiner goes on to relay that Adam and Eve were actually the first human couple, product of alien DNA experimental interbreeding with primates, conducted by the alien race we identify in ancient Sumerian texts as the Annunaki.[7]

The 2000 book *Rex Deus: The True Mystery of Rennes-Le-Chateau and the Dynasty of Jesus,* by Marylin Hopkins, Graham Simmans, and Tim Wallace-Murphy, articulates another shadowy version of hidden blood ties and the theory that the bloodlines of Jesus and Mary were intricately linked to a lineage of 24 high priests of the Temple in Jerusalem. This bloodline was known as the "Rex Deus"—the bloodline of the "Kings of God"[8]—and ties to all the fantastical stories of King Solomon possessing a ring with which he could control demonic elements to aid in the building of the temple, as well as connections to the masons.

These few mentioned works represent only a small number of the host of fictional, non-fiction, and documentary books and films released on this topic since the 1980s. But they illustrate a fact: Enough evidentiary material exists to establish a case for such claims, which are not at all far-fetched nor gymnastics of the imagination. Simply consider the biblical Jesus of Nazareth and his first recorded public miracle, launching his public ministry, the Wedding at Cana.

In the biblical account, Jesus is in attendance at a local wedding of some person left unnamed and unmentioned in the passage. In the account, recorded in the Gospel of John 2:1–11, Jesus' mother (her name, Mary, omitted from the passage) rushes up to Jesus in a bit of panic, telling Jesus that the party is out of wine, to which Jesus says, in what seems a rather brusque reply, "O Woman, what have I to do with you? My hour has not yet come." His mother then says to the servants to do whatever Jesus tells them. Jesus then orders them to take all the empty pitchers and fill them with water, and to draw out some and take it to the chief steward waiter. After tasting it, and not knowing where it came from, the steward congratulated the bridegroom on departing from the custom of serving the best wine first by serving it last (John 2:6–10). John adds: "Jesus did this, the first of his signs, in Cana of Galilee and it revealed his glory and his disciples believed in him."

> "[1–3]Three days later there was a wedding in the village of Cana in Galilee. Jesus' mother was there. Jesus and his disciples were guests also. When they started running low on wine at the wedding banquet, Jesus' mother told him, "They're just about out of wine." [4]Jesus said, "Is that any of our business, Mother— yours or mine? This isn't my time. Don't push me." [5]She went ahead anyway, telling the servants, "Whatever he tells you, do it." [6–7]Six stoneware water pots were there, used by the Jews for ritual washings. Each held twenty to thirty gallons. Jesus ordered the servants, "Fill the pots with water." And they filled them to the brim. [8]"Now fill your pitchers and take them to the host," Jesus said, and they did. [9–10]When the host tasted the water that had become wine (he didn't know what had just happened but the servants, of course, knew), he called out to the bridegroom, "Everybody I know begins with their finest wines and after the guests have had their fill brings in the cheap stuff. But you've saved the best till now!" [11]This act in Cana of Galilee was the first sign Jesus gave, the first glimpse of his glory. And his disciples believed in him."
> (John 2:1–11)

My speculative contention is that this wedding is the wedding of Jesus. There are a few things to note in this passage that would tend to establish this fact. First, in first-century Judea, it was a Jewish tradition (tantamount to law) that a rabbi must be a married man in order to be worth his salt and effective in his ministry. This miracle represents the first miracle of Jesus' public ministry. Second, in first-century Judea (as well as in modern times) it was Jewish custom and tradition for the groom's family to provide the wine for the wedding. In this passage you see Jesus' mother approaching him under some stress that the wedding has no wine. Why did she approach Jesus, and why did she seem to have some position of authority at the wedding? Was Jesus, perhaps, the groom? Finally we see Jesus (the groom?) ordering the servants and presenting the wedding with wine.

Perhaps the text of the passage, as with so many other passages in the Bible, is presenting certain facts and omitting others, or completely redirecting the actual events to point in a different direction. As we know, the early Church fathers had specific views they needed to convey in order to establish Church practice and governance, and the repression of women in any position of authority seemed to govern the effort. For Jesus to have been married would have elevated a woman to a lofty role, so they deleted the wedding and reduced Mary Magdalene to the role of prostitute, which is never stated anywhere in the biblical text. Pope Gregory the Great's homily on Luke's gospel dated September 14, 591, first suggested that Mary Magdalene was a prostitute: "She whom Luke calls the sinful woman, whom John calls Mary, we believe to be the Mary from whom seven devils were ejected according to Mark. And what did these seven devils signify, if not all the vices? ... It is clear, brothers, that the woman previously used the unguent to perfume her flesh in forbidden acts"(homily XXXIII).[9]

Speculative as my theory may be, it is clearly apparent that the Church and many denominations overtly suppress the role of important women in the scriptures, with few exceptions, and just as overtly—even vehemently—resist the notion that Jesus could have been a married man who produced offspring. One old Bible school friend of mine reacted quite harshly at this notion when I presented it, insisting that marriage and children would invalidate the divinity of Jesus Christ. When I asked him why, he fumbled for an intelligent answer but could provide none, reverting simply to stating that my words were heretical. And, in truth, if Jesus Christ is indeed divinity, "God very God," does not the New Testament tell us that he experienced life and was "tempted in all points, just as we are, yet without committing sin" (Hebrews 4:15)?

The big question that remains unanswered is this: Did Yeshua bar Joshof, Jesus of Nazareth, called the Christ, marry and father a child? And if he did, was that child the beginning of a bloodline that could be traced or discovered, and did it merge into the ruling class of the Merovingian kings?

As the theory goes, Jesus married Mary of Magdala, a woman from whom he cast out seven demons (thought to be seven illnesses and infirmities) and who became one of his most ardent disciples, even to the point where after Jesus' death, resurrection, and ascension, she was referred to by the other disciples and followers of Jesus as Miriamne, "The Great Teacher." According to the non-canonical Gospel of Phillip, a Gnostic Gospel of the New Testament apocrypha (dating to the third century), Mary Magdalene was revered as the Great Teacher, establishing her as the heir-apparent to the living philosophies of Jesus. Her husband.

> There were three who always walked with the Lord: Mary, his mother, and her sister, and Magdalene, the one who was called his companion. His sister and his mother and his companion were each a Mary. (the Gospel of Phillip)

There is another passage from the Gospel of Phillip referring to Mary Magdalene, but as is common with millennia-old documents, it is incomplete due to damage to the original manuscript, and several words are missing. The best, scholarly guesses as to what they were are shown here in brackets. Most notably—and frustratingly—there is a hole in the manuscript after the phrase *and used to kiss her often on her....* The passage appears to be telling of Jesus *kissing* Mary Magdalene, and Jesus goes on to use a parable to explain to the disciples why he loved her more than he loved them:

> As for the Wisdom who is called "the barren," she is the mother
> of the angels. And the companion of [the saviour was Mar]
> y Ma[gda]lene. [Christ loved] M[ary] more than [all] the
> disci[ples, and used to] kiss her [softly] on her [hand]. The rest
> of [the disciples were offended by it and expressed disapproval].
> They said to him "Why do you love her more than all of us?"
> The Saviour answered and said to them, "Why do I not love
> you like her? When a blind man and one who sees are both
> together in darkness, they are no different from one another.
> When the light comes, then he who sees will see the light, and
> he who is blind will remain in darkness."

However, the word *hand* is not necessarily the word after *kiss her... on her....* It may have been cheek, forehead, lips, or feet to simply show respect.[10]

The holy bloodline of Jesus is nothing more than a theory, filled with speculative evidences and magnificent stories, but, as with other theories of this sort, it is filled with conjecture, filler content, and unsustainable facts. The theory goes on to state that Jesus Christ had a natural child with Mary Magdalene, named Sarah (Hebrew for "princess"), who was then taken to France to keep her safe, either during Magdalene's pregnancy or as a young child. It is Sarah's blood descendants who in later centuries founded the Merovingian dynasty of the early kings of France.

The theory goes on to state that a secret order protects these royal claimants because they may be the literal descendants of Jesus and his wife, Mary Magdalene, or, at the very least, of King David and the High Priest Aaron. This secret society known as the Priory of Sion has a long and illustrious history dating back to the First Crusade, starting with the creation of the Knights Templar as its military and financial front. The Priory is said to be led by a Grand Master—or "Nautonnier," one who steers through murky waters—and is devoted to reestablishing the Merovingian dynasty on the hereditary thrones of Europe and Jerusalem.

Historically speaking, the Roman Catholic Church is said to have attempted to exterminate all remnants of this dynasty as well as their guardians, the Cathars and the Templars, during the Inquisition. Their goal, according to Jesus conspiratorialists, was to maintain power through the apostolic succession of Peter instead of the hereditary succession of Mary Magdalene—so the mythos goes.

A variation on the bloodline theory is that Jesus didn't die on the cross but survived the torturous event, after which he fled to Kashmir, returning to Srinagar, where he had originally been influenced by Buddhist teachings. It was there that he died of old age, and the biblical accounts of his resurrection were enhanced by his followers. This theory is given merit by close comparisons of the teachings of Jesus in the Gnostic Gospel of St. Thomas paralleling classical Buddhist Sutras. The theory also has parallels with other stories of Jesus' disciples fleeing to foreign lands, such as the journey of Joseph of Arimathea to England after the death of Jesus, taking with him a piece of thorn from Jesus' crown of thorns, which he planted on Weayall Hill in Glastonbury, England. The tree that grows there, across the valley from Glastonbury Tor, is said to be a direct descendent of the tree that sprouted from the thorn planted by Joseph, and a flowering sprig is sent to the monarch of England every Christmas, a tradition started during the reign of James I, royal sponsor of the 1611 King James Bible, in the early 1600s.

The Beast From the Sea

Buried in obscure antiquity, there is a legend surrounding Meroveus, the founder of the Merovingian dynasty, in which he made claims to having been sired by two different fathers. Despite the more recent claims that the Merovingians descended from the bloodlines of Jesus Christ (predicated, of course, on the notion that Jesus was indeed married to Mary Magdalene and fathered a child with her who carried on his lineage in ancient France), King Clodian, the human father of Meroveus, and a strange beast of the sea were the progenitors of the first Merovingian king. Meroveus's mother was already pregnant with her son by King Clodion when she went swimming in the surf and encountered the beast of the sea.

> "Despite the carefully listed genealogies of his time, the heritage of *Meroveus* was strangely obscured in the monastic annals. Although the rightful son of Clodion, he was nonetheless said by the historian Priscus to have been *sired by an arcane sea creature, the Bistea Neptunis....*

> "The Sicambrian Franks, from whose female line the Merovingians emerged were associated with Grecian Arcadia before migrating to the Rhineland. As we have seen, they called themselves the *Newmage*—'People of the New Covenant', just as the Essenes of Qumran had once been known. It was the Arcadian legacy that was responsible for the *mysterious* sea beast—the *Bistea Neptunis*—as symbolically defined in the Merovingian ancestry. The relevant sea-lord was King Pallas, a god of old Arcadia. His predecessor was the great Oceanus. The immortal sea-lord was said to be 'ever-incarnate in a dynasty of ancient kings' whose symbol was a fish—as was the traditional symbol of Jesus"

> —Laurence Gardner, *Bloodline of the Holy Grail*
> (author's emphasis throughout)

The *Bistea Neptunis*[11] was worshipped in classical antiquity as the Roman god Neptune and as Poseidon in Greek mythology. Neptune was the mythological god of the sea who is said to have founded Atlantis, which is the pagan version of the antediluvian civilization that existed prior to the Great Flood of Noah, in which God wipes out all of humanity while purging the earth of the Nephilim, the offspring of the Elohim, in Genesis chapter seven.

In the Apostle John's visions on the Isle of Patmos, he records an image of the Antichrist as the beast that rises out of the sea. This appearance of the *Bistea Neptunis* in the Book of Revelation has interesting linkages to the Merovingian legend, especially in light of the fact that the Merovingian monarchs are said to have demonic connections.

> [1]And I stood upon the sand of the sea, and saw a beast rise up out of the sea, having seven heads and ten horns, and upon his horns ten crowns, and upon his heads the name of blasphemy. [2]And the beast which I saw was like unto a leopard, and his feet were as the feet of a bear, and his mouth as the mouth of a lion: and the dragon gave him his power, and his seat, and great authority.
> (Revelation 13:1–2)

The name Meroveus is a name created from two conjoined French words: *mer*, meaning "sea," and *vere*, meaning "werewolf" or "dragon"—hence, beast from the sea. The Book of Revelation refers to the dragon in specific terms as being none other than Satan, the devil.

> And there was war in heaven: Michael and his angels fought against the dragon; and the dragon fought and his angels....
> And the great dragon was cast out, that old serpent, called the Devil, and Satan, which deceiveth the whole world: he was cast out into the earth, and his angels were cast out with him.
> (Revelation 12:9)

It is interesting to make note at this spot regarding two comparatives that stand out in this Merovingian mythology. The first is the relation to the great beast who rises up out of the sea. In the Sumerian mythology of Enki/Ea, it is said that he is the Lord of the Earth and the Lord of the Abzu, that great underworld sea, atop of which lay the Snake Marsh. It is the connectivity to the snake that the second comparative comes into view: the Dragon, which is simply an archaic derivative of the snake and the ancient serpent.

Some of the books mentioned (*Bloodline of the Holy Grail; Holy Blood, Holy Grail;* and *The Da Vinci Code*) were popular books marketed for mass consumption and sold millions of copies. As such, conspiratorialists hold them up as being nothing less than propaganda tools that conceal the true origins of the Merovingian race. This propaganda is obviously something masterminded from behind the mystical scenes in the mists of demonic and otherworldly ether. For their esoteric allusion to the Merovingians' legendary progenitor, King Meroveus, having been sired by a mysterious beast of the sea, is an overt claim that the bloodlines of the Merovingians were of literal satanic descent. The demonic origins and history of the Merovingian Dynasty, also known as the Dragon Dynasty in honor of the great red dragon (the "pendragon") of Revelation 12 and 13, are revealed in less available insider sources such as Gardner's *Realm of the Ring Lords* and *Kenneth Grant and the Merovingian Mythos* (published by DragonKey Press).

The Tuatha dé Danann

In Irish mythology, it is said that a race of kings descended from the heavens to the ancient Celts of Ireland. These tall, bright, shining creatures were elegant and beautiful, and brought with them the secret knowledge of the gods. Although the Tuatha represent a caste of Irish elemental beings, there are also accounts of them being flesh and blood conquerors of the Fir Bolg, one of the more ancient races inhabiting Ireland, coming down and invading from the four northern cities of Falias, Gorias, Murias, and Finias, where they acquired their occult skills and magical attributes.[12]

169

Tuatha dé Danann roughly, but imprecisely translates as "peoples'/ children of the goddess Danu." In the old Irish *tuath* means "people, tribe, nation"; *dé* is the genitive case of *día,* meaning "god, goddess, supernatural being, object of worship."[13] They are often referred to simply as the Tuatha, Tua, or the Tuatha dé, which also was used in early Irish Christian texts as a name for the Israelite diaspora.[14] That, in and of itself, is an interesting historical reference: As Danu has also been rendered Anu, the reference—if not already obvious—creates an interesting link between Israel and ancient Sumerian mythology.

According to *Lebor Gabála Érenn* (*The Book of the Taking of Ireland*), the Middle Irish title of a loose collection of poems and prose narratives recounting the mythical origins and history of the Irish from the creation of the world down to the Middle Ages, they descended to Ireland "in dark clouds" and "landed on the mountains of Conmaicne Rein in Connacht, bringing a darkness over the sun for three days and three nights."[15] In another version of the story, less steeped in the mistiness of legend, the Tuatha landed in a fleet of sea vessels on the shores of what is modern-day Connemara, Ireland. As if to seal their resolve, they burned all their ships, so as to provide themselves no mode of retreat. The rising smoke from the fires is said to be the basis for the myth that says they arrived in smoke from the skies.

A poem in the Lebor Gabála *Érenn* says of their arrival:

> It is God who suffered them, though He restrained them
> They landed with horror, with lofty deed,
> In their cloud of mighty combat of spectres,
> Upon a mountain of Conmaicne of Connacht.
> Without distinction to discerning Ireland,
> Without ships, a ruthless course
> The truth was not known beneath the sky of stars,
> Whether they were of heaven or of earth.[16]

After a series of wars, it is said that the Tuatha dé Danann receded into the Hollow Hills and eventually became known as the Elven folk of Cletic lore. It is interesting to note that the "El" of Elven is a derivative of the ancient Sumerian Elil and the Hebrew Elohim. The connectivity between the mythological Tuatha dé Danann and the Nephilim is well worth recognition, as they are perhaps etymological descendants in the same vein, again, as Elil and Ea are to Elohim and YWHW.

On a literary note, the Tuatha dé Danann are the basis for J.R.R. Tolkein's tall, elegant, bright, shining Elven people of Lothlorien. Tolkein had his finger on the pulse of shadowy history, and was obviously on to something.

Tuatha dé Annunaki?

"...The ancient people of the Tuatha De Danann...were the supernatural tribe of the pre-Achaean agricultural goddess Danae of Argos, or perhaps of the Aegean mother-goddess, Danu. But their true name rendered in its older form was Tuadhe d'Anu. As such, they were the people (or tribe) of Anu, the great sky god of the Annunaki."

—Sir Laurence Gardner, *Realm of the Ring Lords:*
The Myths and Magic of the Grail Quest

The Canaanite territory of northern Israel is said to have once been occupied by the Israelite tribe of Dan, who, during the days of the Bible's Great Exodus, around 1446 BCE, is said to have separated from Moses and the rest of the Israelites, traveling to the north. There the Dannites encountered the worship of Baal/Pan and became involved in the pagan fertility rites practiced by the indigenous Canaanite peoples at Mount Hermon, the very place where, according to the Book of Enoch, the Sons of God descended to the earth and made a pact to go in among human women and have children with them, bequeathing the Nephilim.

171

The people of the Israelite tribe of Dan intermingled with the Canaanite Tuatha dé Danann, also known as the Dragon Lords of Anu, said to be the offspring of the ancient Sumerian Annunaki. This is also one of the interpretations of the "Sons of God" intermingling with the "daughters of men," referenced in the Genesis chapter six story of the Nephilim. One of the human-based interpretations of the story is that the children of Israel, as represented by the tribe of Dan, broke the law of God and intermarried with the Canaanites in the region of Mount Hermon, where the Elohim were said to have descended. Cultural values of the day did not allow for the women of Israel to intermingle with the men of another culture, so only the men were said to have taken Canaanite brides from the Tuatha dé Danann. Hence, the basis of the story for the Sons of God intermingling with the daughters of men. From there, the integrated tribe a Dan and Dannan/Danu/Anu migrated to the north and west, settling along the way in the European and Scandinavian regions as a conquering nomadic people, replacing those they conquered with their own traditions blended with the Canaanite Annunaki Serpent culture.[17]

I again find the similarities and connectivities staggering: Tuatha dé Danann, Danites, Tribe of Dan, and their linkage to the Dragon Lords, the Annunaki, and the Serpent. Are these simply tricks of word similarities, or are the coincidences far too great to overlook?

Yet another version of the origins of the Tuatha dé Danann, the Dragon Lords of the Anu (before settling in Ireland around 800 BCE), is that they were the descendents of the Black Sea princes of Scythia,[18] now known as the Ukraine. Like the original dynastic Pharaohs, they traced their ancestry to the great Pendragons (note: Uther and Arthur Pendragon of the Arthurian legends) of Mesopotamia, and from them sprang the kingly lines of the ancient Britons, the Irish Bruithnigh, and the Picts, the indigenous people of northern Scotland. In Wales the

Tuatha founded the Royal House of Gwynedd, whereas in Cornwall in the southwest of England, they were the sacred gentry known as Pict-Sidhe, connected with the early Merlin (Myrddin) and Tyntagel, the legendary Cornish birthplace of King Arthur.

> "So, from a single caste of the original Blood Royal—whether known as the Sangréal, the Albi-gens or the Ring Lords—we discover many of the descriptive terms which sit at the very heart of popular folklore. For here, in this one noble race, we have the 'elves', 'fairies' and 'pixies'—not beguiling little folk, but distinguished Kings and Queens of the Dragon succession."
>
> —Sir Laurence Gardner, *Realm of the Ring Lords*

The Psalter of Cashel (the lost Book of Munster) states: "[T]he Tuatha dé Danann' ruled in Ireland for about two centuries, and were highly skilled in architecture and other arts from their long residence in Greece."[19] According to The Psalter of Cashel, the Tuatha dé Danann were regarded as the descendants of Danaus, the son of Belus, who went with his 50 daughters to Argos, the home of his ancestral Io. In Irish legends the Tuatha dé Danann, considered to be demi-gods, were said to have possessed a Grail-like vessel.[20] They were teachers of ancient wisdom and the founders of the Druidic priesthood.

As you can see, mythology melds with history. In the vaguely historical, mostly pseudo-anthropological works of Sitchin, the Annunaki are space travelers who descended in linguistically forced "firey rockets." In anthropological research, they are the deified kings of the ancient Sumerians whose descendants migrated north to Black Sea region and south to Palestine, encountering other ancient peoples, and merging cultures and language.

In a Merovingian sense—and in accordance with modern Reptilian mythology—these are the ancestral Euro-Semitic people who forged the bloodlines of the royal families of the Franks, not to mention the royal houses of Europe's history.

The Holy Grail

The Holy Grail has for centuries been linked to the legends of King Arthur and his Knights of the Round Table. It was a quest on which the mythical king sent his mighty men of valor. In more modern interpretations, this grail quest has been seen as less a quest for an object (the cup of Jesus used at the last supper) but one of finding and identifying the bloodline of Jesus Christ, the holy Son of God who was the divine savior of humanity. Take into consideration the aforementioned migration of the Tuatha dé Danann, and their purported establishment of the royal lines of Wales and Cornwall, both of which have connectivity to the Arthurian legends, and you will see the linkage between the legendary quest for the grail and the quest for the blood heirs of Jesus. Yet the dynastic lines of kings who claim to have descended from this hidden bloodline were not any part of the Christianity we recognize today. They were known as Sorcerer Kings and Dragon Lords, some of whom claimed to be not only descendants of the bloodline of Jesus Christ, but also the Luciferian bloodline, which seems an outright contradiction to the former!

The Merovingian kings were said to have descended from the Atlantian diaspora, the remnant of inhabitants of Atlantis who had escaped the destruction of that mythological region, fleeing to the Pyrenees Mountain region, bringing with them their abilities as occult adepts, and practitioners of arcane sciences and the esoteric arts. The Merovingians, in fact, were often called Sorcerer Kings, or thaumaturge kings—sorcerers, workers of miracles, and practitioners of the black arts.[21] These are the descendants of the grail, the heirs of the bloodline of the Christ.

These are the things that delve into the darker side of Judeo-Christian history and lore—the mysteries of God, if you will—and they end up painting God in a very different light than we were taught in Sunday School or Synagogue, which is why they are deemed as heretical and blasphemous to the Church. But what if they are true? How would this affect your faith or your adherence to what you believed you knew from the Bible? Or would it simply send you back into those pages to dig deeper for answers, perhaps even into prayer to ask if that Holy God is truly there in the form you once understood Him?

Digging into more rabbinic lore, there is another version of the story of Cain, the son of Eve, in which he was not the son of Adam (which we've already established several times over, between this book and *The Rise and Fall of the Nephilim*), but of the fallen angel Samael, whose name loosely equates to Lucifer. We have already established, textually speaking, that the Serpent in the Garden was a character called Nachash, in accordance with the Hebrew of the Genesis text. But according to this obscure rabbinic version of this particular bit of Hebrew lore, it was Samael who appeared to Eve as the Serpent, the Nachash, seducing her. Whoever it was who actually appeared as the Serpent isn't as important as is the fruit of that union: Eve's firstborn twin son, Cain. If the Merovingians knew of this rabbinic version of the story—which they no doubt did—it could have been the basis of their alleged assertion that they possessed, flowing in their bodies, the blood of both Christ and Lucifer. And the idea that Cain was the offspring of a superior intelligence was already a well-established teaching of the Cainite Gnostics, of which the Merovingians were also sure to have intimate knowledge.

An alternate version of the Cain saga, equally Luciferian in its connotations, says that he was the son of Adam's first wife, Lilith, who was also a candidate for the Serpent, Nachash, in the Garden of Eden.[22] According to rabbinic lore, she had been the consort of Elohim before

175

her fall from grace and descent to the earth. It is interesting that, of the two alternate traditions concerning Cain's parentage, both involve a Luciferian-Elohim bloodline connection.

The Lilith-Samael version of the story also bears great connectivity to the grail saga insofar as, according to this account, the angelic/demonic pairing produces a son of their *own* who seems to play a recurring role in the entire grail mythos: Asmodeus. Not only is Asmodeus said to have played the central role in building the Temple of Solomon, the edifice from which the Knights Templar took their name, but he is also represented in the dominant statue at the entrance to Rennes-le-Chateau in France, which has enormous legendary connections to the grail mythos. The recurrence of the character of Asmodeus in connection to grail lore gives credence to the notion that both he and the descendants of Cain may in fact have shared kindred ancestry. In some traditions it has been said that it was Asmodeus, not God, whom Moses called upon to part the Red Sea. Though portrayed as a demon or devil figure, the name Asmodeus reveals that he may not always have been viewed as such, for Asmodeus translates simply to Lord God (*Ashma* = "Lord," and *Deus* = "God"). Asmodeus bears the same brand of duality found in the serpent deities of ancient Egypt, Sumar, and myriad other cultures we have mentioned in this book—which happen to be only the tip of the iceberg. So, again, we have to ask ourselves what it is we think we really, truly know for sure.

On an even more intriguing observance are the four French words positioned above the sculpture of Asmodeus at the entrance to Rennes-le-Chateau: "PARCE SIGNE TULE VAINCRAS." These four letters are an anagramic code in Latin, "CELATA AGNI SUPER ENRICVS" ("LAMB'S SECRET OVER ENRICUS"). "Lamb" is a reference to Jesus Christ, and it is thought that this phrase over the sculpture of Asmodeus is the third of a series of encoded anagrams that speak to the location of the Holy Grail. (To rabbit trail into that topic here would be lengthy and worthy of a book all its own, so for now, consider it fodder for thought and exploration.)

Another possible origin of the Luciferian bloodline theory is inextricably linked to the Elohim, the pantheon of gods in mythology who said in the Book of Genesis: "Come, let Us make man in Our image." Elohim is the plural form for the name of God: "God Among Many Gods," the bene ha Elohim, the "Sons of God" known as the Watchers in the Book of Enoch.

We have already established that the word *Elohim* is an etymological descendent of the name Elil, chief god of the Annunaki of the Sumerian culture, but it also has roots in the ancient Babylonian word *Ellu,* which means "shining ones." This phrase has a distinctively Luciferian connotation, because the name Lucifer literally means "light bearer." Additionally, if you see Lucifer as being the same person as Nachash in the Genesis account of the Garden of Eden, remember that Nachash, by definition means, "crafty magician, *illuminator, bright shining one.*" It is also to be noted that the descendants of Cain, who became the deified kings of Sumer, bore the title of Ari, a term that also meant "shining ones." And as I have already contended, Cain being the son of Nachash and Eve, is the first of the Nephilim mentioned in the Book of Genesis. The phrase *shining ones* would be a very apt description for the descendants of Enoch's Watchers (the Sons of God of the Genesis account), who were said to have, according to the Enochian account, "hair white as snow, pale eyes, and pale skin that filled the room with light" (Enoch 105:10).

The Sumerian Ari are almost always depicted as wearing crowns bearing horns, and some of their descendants were said actually to have had horns. For instance, the most famous statue of Moses, carved by Michelangelo, depicts him with horns atop his forehead, not wholly inappropriate for someone who may be a blood relation of Asmodeus. But we also must consider the anti-Semitism of medieval Europe, a time of great bigotry against Jews and Hebrew culture. Many Christian artists in Europe, especially under the power of the Vatican papacy, were "required" to depict their biblical Jewish subjects as having horns, in accordance with the opinions of the powers that be. So, the presence of horns on the statuary heads of patriarchal Jews from the Bible had, some say, absolutely nothing to do with the mystical. They were a political contrivance. Theologians protest that they are not horns, merely rays of light. If they are rays of light, it could also suggest a Luciferian subtext, due to the bright shining element of Nachash and the Elohim.

Tetradrachm of Lysimachos. The head of Alexander is featured wearing royal and divine symbols: the diadem and the horns of Zeus Ammon. C. 305–281 BC. Image made available through Wikimedia Commons.

It's obvious, even to the casual observer, that they are *indeed* horns, which is not at all inconsistent with the normal medieval Western depiction of Moses and other biblical patriarchs, based on the description of

Moses' face as *cornuta* ("horned") in the Latin Vulgate translation of Exodus. The Douay-Rheims Bible translates the Vulgate as: *"And when Moses came down from the mount Sinai, he held the two tables of the testimony, and he knew not that his face was **horned** from the conversation of the Lord"* [author's emphasis]. This was, however, a mistranslation of the original Hebrew text, which uses a term equivalent to "radiant," suggesting an effect like a halo. The Greek Septuagint translates the verse as: *"Moses knew not that the appearance of the skin of his face was glorified."*

> **Anecdotal Historical Fact:** Alexander the Great declared himself the Son of God, and he, too, was rumored to have horns. In fact, to this very day, if you talk to people on the streets of Iran (who have a cultural remembrance of his invasion as though it happened last week), they will tell you in all solemnity that it's a historical fact that Alexander had horns, which is why he wore his hair long—to cover them up. There was an ancient Greek coin, the silver tetradrachmon, issued posthumously in the name of Alexander the Great around 242/241 BCE, depicting Alexander with the horns of Ammon-Ra.

Cain, the first of the twin-born sons of Eve, seems to have engendered his own traditional stories, as found in an obscure Gnostic sect bearing his name called the Cainites. Like the Carpocrateans, the salvific doctrine of the Cainites espoused a theology that declared the believer must gain favor with God by "making the journey through everything."[23] Fourth-century Bishop of Salamis St. Epiphanius describes the Gnostic Cainites as a group of believers who possessed an "obscure chaos of evil practices,"[24] "consecrating...lustful or illegal acts to various heavenly beings...heretics so adulterated with the dualism...and licentious practices of Oriental heathenism..."[25] as a sort of sacred prerequisite.

Interestingly, many contemporary scholars compare them to Satanists, but that was a common thought already forming nearly 2,000 years ago. In alignment with our study of the Nephilim and the serpentine cultures, Cainites also taught that Eve's twin sons had different fathers, purporting that Cain was the offspring of Eve by a superior power, and Abel was Eve's son by an inferior power. The Cainites are also considered an heretical group as they possessed the Gospel of Judas, in which Judas is written as the disciple who "studied the mysteries of God," and that his knowledge was so much more advanced than any of the other disciples of Jesus, that he, in adherence to the insistence of Jesus himself, betrayed Jesus to the Jewish Sanhedrin so that the prophecy would be fulfilled.[26] In disparity to the accepted gospels contained in the canonical Bible, Judas did this out of complete altruistic discipleship to his master, resulting in such a tumultuous grief that he committed suicide. And as a result of his loyalty to Jesus, his name has been besmirched in Christianity for all time.

Coat of arms of Stenay. Image copyright of the author.

The extent to which the Merovingians knew of these alternate traditions is uncertain. Whether or not they believed in them is more uncertain still, yet it remains likely that they both knew about these traditions and took them quite seriously. To this very day, the coat of arms of the capital of the Merovingian empire, Stenay, bears an image of the devil. And the original name of Stenay was Satanicum.

How the Merovingians Influenced Hilter

In 1919, at the age of 30, Adolf Hitler joined the occultist Germanic Revivalist Thule Society,[27] although there are no historical records indicating that he ever attended a single meeting.[28] Hitler later reconceived and organized this organization into the National Socialist German Workers' Party, better known as the Nazi Party. The Thule Society was founded a year earlier by the followers of two men: Jorg Lanz Von Liebenfels, who later claimed that it was his "occultist ideals" that helped form Hilter's thinking,[29] and Guido von List, a Viennese "Renaissance Man" of many varied interests and talents who gained his popular notoriety as an occultist and *völkisch* ("ethnic folk") author. Through his writings and popular approach to reviving Germanic mysticism, List was one of the original New Agers, establishing himself as an important contributor to what has been hailed as modern Germanic revivalism. He was a late-19th-century pioneer in Runic Revivalism and Runosophy, a specialized branch of archaic Germanic linguistics not only used as a means to establish Germanic foundations in ancient language transmission, but also steeped in a mysticism that purported the proper usage of runes could divine, charm, prognosticate, curse, and even bring people back from the dead. List was a Pagan occultist to the heart, and by later standards was the poster child for the colloquial term *long hair*. Perhaps his runic forays worked well for him, for he was highly regarded by the people, who saw his particular brand of folk writing as a solid foundation to the reemergence of Germany as a substantial power in the West.

So much can be said on these matters that a veritable tome could be written on these topics alone. Suffice it for the purposes of this study to say that the Thule Society, though outwardly deemed a populace organization that lent pride to the growing nationalist movement in Germany—rather like a grown-up version of the American Boy Scouts—became the animus behind the organizing of what was known as the *Deutsche Arbeiterpartei (DAP)*, a German workers' party that met in local beer halls and was made up of members who wanted to see a rise in the worker class.

Adolf Hitler's DAP membership card, with the forged date and number, reduced from 555 to 55 to make him appear as if he were an original founder and member. Image by Mike Peel www.mikepeel.net. *Made available through Wikimedia Commons.*

Hitler, who at that time was a corporal in the German army, was ordered to attend a meeting of the DAP in order to spy on them for the purposes of establishing their political agenda. While he was at this meeting, he did what a good spy ought not do by getting into a rather violent political argument with a member of the group. In short, he was recognized for his oratory skills and later invited to become a member of the fairly unorganized party. Hitler agreed to join and began to organize the party from what was tantamount to a bunch of guys meeting at the pub to argue politics into a solid organization. Hitler renamed the organization the National Socialist German Workers' Party (NSDAP)—the Nazi Party. According to Hitler biographer Ian Kershaw, the Thule's "membership list...reads like a Who's Who of early Nazi sympathizers and leading figures in Munich,"[30] with its small membership list inclusive of such historical German figures as Rudolf Hess, Gottfried Feder, Alfred Rosenberg, Hans Frank, Julius Lehmann, Karl Harrer, and Dietrich Eckart.[31]

By today's standards, the Thule Society's underlying philosophy would be considered heinous in concept and societally scorned in intent. At the core of the Thule was their occultist belief in the origins of a superior man, the Aryan race. In 1917, this underlying theme of superiority extended to membership qualifications. If you wanted to join the society, you were required to sign a special "blood declaration of faith" establishing lineage: "The signer hereby swears to the best of his knowledge and belief that no Jewish or coloured blood flows in either his or in his wife's veins, and that among their ancestors are no members of the coloured races."[32]

The organizational intent of the Thule was originally an outwardly innocuous German study group headed by Berliner Walter Nauhaus, a wounded World War I veteran turned art student. In 1918, Nauhaus came into contact with a occultist named Rudolf von Sebottendorf, the newly elected head of the Bavarian Germanenorden Walvater of the Holy Grail,[33] an offshoot organization formed after a schism with the Thule Society. Nauhaus and Sebottendorf became associates while recruiting for their particular branches, and eventually they merged their branches under the Thule name, using it as a cover name for Sebottendorff's Munich lodge of the Germanenorden Walvater. Not only are we starting to see all the occultist roots to the Thule and its varying offshoots and chapters, but also the growing chimera of political power. What started in occultist folk nationalistic revitalization quickly turned populace and aggressively political in intent and heinously evil in philosophy.

The Thule Society seal. Image from proswastika.org/e107_iamges/custom/ thulegesellschaft_emblem.jpg.

The occultist origins of Nazi Aryanism, specifically as influenced by the Thule's philosophical foundation, is deeply probed in Kevin

184

Abrams's and Scott Lively's *The Pink Swastika*. Abrams and Lively document how the Thule Society relied on ancient occultist supernaturalism to imbue their members with powers to be used for their Aryan claims and the foundational thinking behind their belief in the use of eugenics.[34] The fire of Adolf Hitler's dream of an Aryan super-race was fueled by the underlying occult theology of the Thule Society. Adhering to the belief that they were somehow infused with esoteric powers passed on to them by the spirits of the lost civilization of Atlantis, members of the society regarded themselves as metaphysically imbued with the god-like wisdom of these advanced ancients, fueling them to create a new race of Aryan super-men. They followed a more-or-less Darwinian philosophy that moved them by some esoteric "eminent domain" to claim superiority and eliminate the 'inferior' races.[35]

Jorg Lanz Von Liebenfels, the spiritual inspiration behind the founding of the Thule Society, was a Cistercian monk who claimed to have been given revelation and enlightenment upon discovering the rune-filled tombstone of a Templar knight. After interpreting what he believed were encoded massages on the tombstone, he began constructing his own philosophies of a blue-eyed/blond-haired, God-ordained Aryan race and its superiority over lower, inferior races. Lanz was hailed the "Father of National Socialism" by Austrian psychologist Wilfried Daim, who in 1958 penned his study of Lanz in *The Man Who Gave Hitler His Ideas*. The book remains a chilling history of the Merovingians and their infiltration of the Catholic Church.

> Like most Merovingian monasteries Glastonbury became a Benedictine Monastery. And the purpose of Merovingian monasteries was "infiltration" based on the belief that the best way to crush the Church was from "within."... There is no doubt in my mind that [the Grail legend] would have been the work of the Cistercians, founded by Benedictine monks as

"the ratchet" for the structural organization of [the Prieuré de] Sion. Joseph of Arimathea is alone associated with the Grail legend and the Quest of the Grail legends, which per Colliers Encyclopedia, are dominated by the mystical symbolism of Cistercians....

More than any heretical Merovingian organizations, the Cistercians personified the banality of evil at its finest. The name Cistercian and of their first monastery, Citeaux derive from Cistus, of the Cistaceae or Rockrose family resembling the wild rose and cultivated in the Mediterranean. The Myrrh with which Mary Magdalene anointed the Body of Jesus also comes from the Cistus family. And they had chosen the Magdalene...assigning her the symbol of the Rose and Cross in memory of the Brotherhood of the Sun founded by Akhenaten who had taken as its symbol the Rose and Cross (Lewis). Cistercians were Rosicrucians. And this Rosicrucian order of monks would triumph in its infiltration of the Church.[36]

The Secret Doctrine, authored by Madam Blavatsky in 1893, became the quintessential sourcebook for 20th-century metaphysical esotericism, and it was heavily influential on the construction of the Thule Society's foundational philosophies. The inner sanctum of the Thule Society was comprised of heavy-hitting occultists, some of whom were overtly Satanist, such as Dietrich Eckart to whom Hitler, very tellingly, dedicated his book, *Mein Kampf.* As a member of the Thule, despite his membership, perchance being in name only, Hitler diligently worked to align himself to the philosophies contained in Blavatsky's *The Secret Doctrine,* the thematic undercurrent of which was that the Aryan root race theory, a gnostic belief that humanity, in its current state of evolution, is destined to be "refined" by something called the seventh root, a belief delineating the philosophy that a race of "godmen," or Homo

Noeticus (the New Man), would rise to preeminence over the rest of humanity, replacing them and cleaning the slate of lesser, races of color and evolutionary inferiority.[37] It has been purported German scientists under the Third Reich, in the development of their war machine and genetic research, were aided by repeated contact with gray entities who came from inside what is known as the hollow earth.

A book considered to be one of the first "science fiction" novels, *Vril, the Power of the Coming Race,* written by Lord Edward Bullwer Lytton and published in 1871 under the original title *The Coming Race,* despite being a fictional book with a Jules Vernes-ish style of 19th-century sci-fi, was highly influential on the thinking of Hitler, the Thule Society, and the Third Reich. Though not Lord Lytton's intention whatsoever, some later Theosophists—the broader field of esotericism founded by Madame Blavatsky—supported the notion that Lord Lytton's book was an actual fictionalized account of an existing superior subterranean master race who utilized the energy-form called Vril. The Thule Society did not merely consider the book the stuff of mid-19th-century science fiction, but, in fact, a true story based on a real magical substance. Helena Blavatsky, the founder of theosophy, endorsed this presupposition in her book *Isis Unveiled* (1877) and again in *The Secret Doctrine* (1888).

So the question that lingers is this: Although Adolf Hitler was clearly an occultist, easily influenced by the mystical and mentally governed by his innate drive to be one of the mythic royalty of the gods and demi-gods of ancient esoterica, was there anything beyond the simplistic interest entailing the influence of any sort of non-human involvement, and if so, was there any linkage to mythical beings that governed his actions? As you have seen, this all funnels backward into the ancient past, linking races, religions, occult practices, and the etymological blending of language blended with the mythologies of ancient religion. And it all goes back to the Annunaki and continued reference to them having Reptilian roots of some sort. Perhaps it is time to go take a soothing bath in the great Abzu, with a fresh rinse in the snake marsh to collect our loose ends and organize our perceptions.

Here and now I have to admit to the fact that I loathe conspiracy theories, for they are generally the stuffs of overactive imaginations spurred into overload upon the discovery of some obscure, ancient myth or legend that they find either substantiates a theory (at least in their own way of thinking), or gives them animus to build a new theory, generally void of historical accuracy, twisting facts and figures, dates, and interpretations of names, events, locations, and archaic religious or occultist practices.

Chapter Seven

The New Age and the Serpent

Make no mistake about it: The mythologies of the Serpent blood-line, though well-established in the past, have never gone away; they've merely morphed into new mythology. We have seen that the Serpent is ever present in antiquity, slithering its way down through history, leaving meandering trails in the dust of nearly every ancient culture and religion, even touching the untouchable spirituality of Jesus Christ and the religion founded by his immediate friends and disciples, proliferated throughout the known world of 2,000 years ago by the evangelist Saul of Tarsus, who after his conversion changed his name to Paul, an apostle who never laid eyes on his master, Jesus Christ, but by vision alone.

The New Age movement, quite frankly, is nothing new, at all, in that it is a revisionist philosophy that has adapted the old mythologies to newer thinking. The notion that we are "all gods" is merely a looping replay of the teachings of the ancients, with the new twist that removes the brother-god/sister-goddess status from only the castes of royals to the common individual. Woven throughout the philosophies, when viewed as an amalgam of religious/spiritual/scientific/metaphysical thinking, is a connectivity to the serpent that is the driving force. One has to consider, only, the prevalent New Age philosophy put forward by well-known teacher and translator Eknath Easwaran,[1] of the kundalini (she who is "ring shaped"), that unconscious, instinctive, or libidinal force or Shakti, that is said to lie coiled at the base of the spine, the "sleeping serpent,"[2] to see where the connection to the Serpent of old has morphed into new meaning, but still maintains its presence.

David Icke

On a more sinister plane, the Serpent takes up abode in the highly conspiratorial world views of David Icke, former British football (that's "soccer" for Yanks like me) star and news/sportscaster turned New Age philosopher, who "exposes the dreamworld we believe to be real"—so says the header on his Website.[3] According to the description on his Amazon.com Author Profile,[4] the elusive Icke says of himself:

David Vaughan Icke (born 4/29/52) British writer and speaker...[describes] himself as the most controversial speaker in the world, he is the author of 19 books and has attracted a global following that cuts across the political spectrum. His 533-page *The Biggest Secret* (1999) has been called "the Rosetta Stone for conspiracy junkies."

Icke was a well-known BBC television sports presenter and spokesman for the Green Party, when in 1990 a psychic told him he was a healer who had been placed on...and that the spirit world was going to pass messages to him so he could educate others. In 1991 he held a press conference to announce that he was a "Son of the Godhead"—a phrase he said later the media had misunderstood.... [Icke] told the BBC's Terry Wogan show that the world would soon be devastated by tidal waves and earthquakes.

...[in] *The Robots' Rebellion* (1994), *And the Truth Shall Set You Free* (1995), *The Biggest Secret* (1999), and *Children of*

the Matrix (2001) [Icke] set out a moral/political worldview
that combined New-Age spiritualism with a passionate
denunciation of totalitarian trends…[in which] many
prominent figures are Reptilian, including George W. Bush,
Queen Elizabeth II, Kris Kristofferson, and Boxcar Willie.

Michael Barkun has described Icke's position as "New Age
conspiracism."… Richard Kahn and Tyson Lewis argue that
the reptilian hypothesis may simply be Swiftian satire, a way of
giving ordinary people a narrative with which to question what
they see around them.

Whenever I encounter self-proclaimed gods and messiahs, despite
their well-meaning messages of peace toward all, unity among fellow
man, and self-growth based on a philosophical foundation that we are
all little gods within the universal collective, I tend to write them off
rather quickly, simply for the self-labeling—good or bad philosophical
beliefs notwithstanding. Be it my past education in theology, or my years
of thinking, writing, and mulling over history, religion, and spirituality,
or simply my exposure to and study of history's cavalcade of messianic
figures who accomplished little other than leading their followers—and
themselves—to bitter ends, it is at the moment of self-proclaimed messianic revelation that I lose interest and cluck my tongue. When I read
that Icke compares himself to a god, substantiated by his many public
appearances and the rare granted interview, I know what he is getting at
from the standpoint of a New Age way of thinking.

Sure, the concept that we are all gods—that we collectively comprise the greater good and have within us the ability to rise to spiritual heights—is not necessarily a thing to be reviled, no matter what
your spirituality or religious (or non-religious) status may be. However,
when those spiritual concepts, not uncommon to many, many religions,
and spiritual trains of thought and practice, are hitched to the wagon of

fringe conspiracy theories that focus on ancient alien Reptilians from another star system, and are working behind the scenes to draw energy off the evil and corruption of humanity, while at the same time pulling the strings behind such mythical groups as the Illuminati, I tend to think the Messiah has stepped off the surface of the water and sunk into the sea of self-adulation entangling himself and his followers in the seaweed of self-deception.

Icke's boiled-down philosophies are not uncommon to the New Age thinking community. He blends staples of the metaphysical discussion about the nature of the universe and consciousness with over-the-top conspiracy theories about public figures ranging from world politicians, religious leaders, and Hollywood celebrities to members of Europe's Royal families. But where he adds a decidedly sinister twist is when he openly accuses them of being Satanic pedophiles, child killers, shape-shifters, mass murderers, serial killers and worse. What seems like unconnected political and social events are in fact, according to Icke, attempts by a hidden Reptilian race to subvert and control humanity.[5]

In his book *The Biggest Secret,* Icke contends that human beings are the product of an extraterrestrial genetic engineering program launched by a race of reptilians called the Annunaki, who came to earth from a solar system in the constellation of Draco. How he makes his connection to Reptilians is as obscure as a few pieces of statuary and a heavy reliance on the works of Zechariah Sitchin. In part, he embraces the ancient Sumerian account of Enki's creation of primeval man as a slave race for the other gods. But he goes beyond merely hailing to ancient mythology as fact, expounding that reality is a holographic experience, the only *true* reality is the realm of the Absolute, which he illustrates by making comparison to the Hollywood movie *The Matrix.*

He teaches a philosophy of Collective Consciousness built on intentionality, reincarnation, a loose, adapted understanding of string theory, and outer-galactic worlds that exist alongside ours on other planes of frequency. He contends that our life experiences alter our DNA by "downloading" new information and "overwriting the software" of our conscious state, and that we are attract experiences to ourselves by means of good and bad thoughts[6]—all in all, a mixture of current metaphysical thought with alien conspiracy theory, and, frankly, very appealing on many levels to those who have been disillusioned by science and religion and are seeking something different to assuage their loneliness or dissatisfaction with the status quo. It is very easy to understand how simply listening to Icke and reading his work can draw one in. His converts are, I am sure, people who have considered both aspects of his foundational thinking, and simply not dug deeply enough to see the missteps and calculated misinterpretations.

David Icke is certainly not the first to have mentioned Reptilian aliens, but he claims he has been the one to have pioneered the road to a better understanding of who the Reptilians really are, and why they continue to interact and influence earthly humans. From secretive governmental control to world domination, ancient religious roots to modern day New Age–ism, Reptilians, according to Icke, *have been known* for their secret agenda. And although we do not have a clear picture of what their true intentions may be, "we are able to gather from history the signs and traces of their past actions and influence with ancient human civilizations. Accounts from the Aztecs, Greeks and Chinese mythology and history leaves us clues as to an ancient race of aliens that perhaps helped and aided the building of our civilizations past and present."[7] He has thrown the ancient alien theory on its head by attributing his particular brand of conspiracy to them.

Icke purports that Reptilians, today, are believed to have shape-shifting abilities that enable them to secretly work their agenda behind the scenes, hidden within the bodies of the ruling classes of Europe and in the majority of U.S. presidents and political figures, not to mention prominent entertainment and pop cultural personages the world over. Icke reports that he has found evidence that our political structure and economic systems have already been influenced by these evil, cunning, crafty (a word used to define Nachash, the serpent character in the Garden of Eden) Reptilians who have worked for thousands of years behind the scenes of human history. These alien intruders, for at least 6,000–8,000 years have seduced, through their cloned counterfeit political leaders and royal personages, the hearts and minds of all humanity, who are blinded to their existence. All the while, these Reptilian overlords are plotting their secret agenda and have been slowly fostering chaos throughout human history, waiting for the right time for the ultimate conquest of our planet.

During his aptly named Turquoise Period, in which Icke and his wife dressed only in the color turquoise due to his claim of some metaphysical effect that acts as a conduit for receiving positive energy, Icke writes that he had been channeling beings from another world and via automatic writing, and had received messages from extraterrestrials telling him that he was a Son of the Godhead—in other words, a "Messiah." After the clamoring controversy and criticisms that ensued after the release of that statement, Icke later attempted to backpedal his statement, amending it and reinterpreting "Son of the Godhead" as the "Infinite Mind."[8] After this experience, in 1990, he met Deborah Shaw, a British psychic living in Calgary, Alberta. Icke began a relationship with Shaw, and the couple had a daughter the next year. Shaw and her infant daughter moved in with Icke and his wife, and she changed her name to Mari Shawsun. Icke's wife changed her name to Michaela, which, she said, was an expression of the Archangel Michael. The eclectic trio was dubbed by the British press as the "turquoise triangle."[9]

You have to think that anyone who predicts the end of the world must be a true believer in his or her ability to prognosticate world event, or have some real deep set faith in his or her ability as a channeler or psychic. Icke made himself part of this short list of doomsayers when he publicly prophesied that the world would end in 1997 (that was, now, 15 years ago, in case you're counting, as of this writing). The end of the world as we knew it, according to Icke, would be preceded by a number of disasters, including a severe hurricane around the Gulf of Mexico and New Orleans—now there's a stretch, a hurricane in the Gulf of Mexico (do I sound too skeptical here?)—volcanic eruptions on the island of Cuba, "disruption" in China, a hurricane in Derry, and an earthquake on the Isle of Arran. He also said in that interview that Los Angeles would become an island, New Zealand would disappear, and the cliffs of Kent would be underwater by Christmas of that year. Icke told reporters that the information contained in this world-ending prophecy had been passed on to him through channeling the voices in his head, which was physically transmitted through automatic writing. As of the writing of this book, Icke is still holding enormous stadium events today, filling sports arenas for his 10-hour conferences. To me, this merely reaffirms my contention, and aptly illustrates the fact that the world is hungry for something and people will look for the things they feel they are missing in any outlet available. When science and religion fail us, we will look to anything to fill the void.

Of course, the end-of-the-world prophecy saw 1997 come and go without incident. Icke later wrote in that he had felt out of control during that press conference where he uttered his prophecy, almost as if he wasn't the one saying the words. He said that he heard his own voice predict the end of the world, yet was completely appalled at what was spilling out of his own mouth: "I was speaking the words, but all the time I could hear the voice of the brakes in the background saying, 'David, what the hell are you saying?'"[10] To Icke's great dismay, his prophecies were splashed all over the front page news the next morning.

In and of themselves, there would seem to be no real harm to Icke's channeling-driven, automatically written script and his alien-Reptilian-overrun world view. If a guy wants to read the works of Zechariah Sitchin and add his own twist, insisting that the Sumerian pantheon of Annunaki gods were a race of Reptile aliens with evil intent, still governing our human affairs from behind a curtain of subterfuge, placing Reptilians in seats of high political world power throughout the ages, imposters in an exterior skin of cloned human flesh, infiltrating their way into all the ruling families of the world, who am I to tell him no? If the man has built a following that buy his books, pays to attend his conferences (and he *is* a phenomenal, eloquent, moving public speaker) and promulgate his views, why should any of us care? If that is the niche David Icke has found to fill his coffers and pay the electric bill, and if people have so little to believe in that they ascribe to his views (which, frankly, I have a hard time believing even Icke himself fully believes) then more power to him. After all, blended throughout his alien message is a more overt call for people to take action against the abuses and oppressions of government, the seeking of world unity in contrast to the New World Order, and the gaining of inner god-like awareness and tranquility. What's so wrong with that? Whatever the vehicle of delivery of the message, the ends justify the means, and if the world becomes a better place, even if we have to foist upon the common mind the notion that if we don't pursue these things, the Reptilians will get a stronger foothold and destroy our world and have us all for lunch. No matter if you are exploiting information and creating a revenue stream, while at the same time foisting peace and unity as the answer, despite how disgusted one might be with his methods, he is ultimately pushing a good thing, right?

But there is a much more insidious aspect to David Icke's assertions. The Reptilians that he claims exist and operate behind the scenes of humanity are ones he links to the bloodlines of Cain, the Merovingians, and the Luciferian lineage. He speaks a form of anti-Semitism, buried in a twisted view of world history, linking the Jews with the Illuminati and the New World Order. The Jews, Icke purports, are the Reptilian-populated, -controlled, -manipulated race seeking world domination through their positions held in the wealthy, ruling, and royal families of Europe and the Western world. The "Chosen People" of the Old Testament are a plague to humanity. And the heinous underpinning of his teachings is that his foundations are laced with historical fact, yet merged into his Reptilian/Illuminati views.

This is not to say that the man does not adhere to good philosophies that stand for the betterment of humanity, but that is the hook that draws an inordinate amount of followers to his philosophies. Truth and fact mixed with bizarre theorizing make for the propagation of a message that is all at once appealing and stimulating to the curious, who are dying for answers to convert our world from what they view as a place of evil and oppression, to one of peace and harmony. Throughout his career, David Icke has professed to having long stood against many political and social systems that may be compromised by the Reptilian alien agenda, and, although Reptilians continue to make their push against humanity, many believe that we have protectors from yet *another* constellation watching their every move and awaiting their chance to move against the Reptilian alien race of aliens and their agenda. Although many of the subjects related to Reptilian aliens or intelligent life elsewhere is usually left to the science-fiction authors and fanatics, David Icke continues to push his own alien agenda toward what he believes to be the "truth that has been hidden from the public for ages."[11]

The Continued Presence of the Serpent

As we have seen throughout this entire book, the presence of the serpent as a thing of both good and evil began as early as the recorded history of humanity and has coursed its meandering trail down through the ages. If, indeed, the imagery and symbolism is a result of ancient humankind's face-to-face encounters with non-human entities in the form of Reptilians, the case of history does not bear out that fact. What we know for a certainty is that the symbolic form of the serpent was inextricably linked with the worship and veneration of the serpent since the dawn of civilization.

Is the presence of the serpent linked to the Luciferian? Does the serpent crawl on its belly solely due to the spoken judgment of God in the Book of Genesis? Or is that simply representative of one version of the serpent in human religion and religious mythology? The seemingly as-yet unanswerable questions are co-dependents with our ability as humans to reach the unreachable and piece the unpierceable. In the vastness of the universe, we are awfully big for our own britches when we think we have the answers to the most elusively quantifiable of questions.

To not know all the answers is the beginning of exploration. That is precisely what I believe we set out to do in all of our sciences, histories, archaeologies, and anthropologies, let alone the verbose pomposity of our philosophies. For me, the pervasive presence of the serpent through our human existence on this planet—our spiritualities, religions, legends, and mythologies—represents an enduring symbol of something or someone that had such great impact on early humanity and their civilizations that it pressed an deeply encoded imprint in our collective psyche that has endured nearly all others, equaled only by our innate need for a deity. Those equally dichotomous quantities have been present with us, family to us, and governing aspects of who and what we are—and surely will continue to be so, prompting further seeking, questing, and digging for the reasons why.

Afterword

It's a river. As you have seen in the preceding pages, the amount of information that stems from one simple thought to the next is filled to over-brimming with tributaries branching off the main artery into other tributaries—stemming into hundreds of branches, little creeks, streams, coolies, and swampy backwaters with inlets and outlets of their own. As I stated at the very start of this book: *"The implications of the comparative historical and religious touch points are so far-reaching that the meanderings of myth one must follow to seek efficacious tendrils of fact could most certainly drive one mad in its contemplation."* It has nearly brought me to that point, not due to the content of the mythologies and varied philosophies, but based upon the overwhelming mountain range of information to sift through and weigh against fact, fiction, insanity, and spirituality—and those distinctions are, sometimes, very difficult to decipher. What is one person's religion is another's folly, leaving plenty of room for criticism, nay-saying, and propagandizing.

There were times in the writing of this little book that I saw myself as a literary version of Meriwether Lewis on his quest to discover the Northwest Passage to the great western Pacific Ocean. After weeks and months of forging through seemingly un-traversable terrain he came, finally, through the foothills and low mountains. It was at that point that Lewis scaled a nearby ridge, certain he would see the Pacific Ocean stretched across the horizon. When he reached the top of the ridge and gazed at what lay beyond, though, all he saw was mile upon mile, range upon range of the craggy, snow-crested Bitterroot Mountains. His spirit sank and he was overcome with the feeling that he'd never find his way. His thoughts of enduring the hardship of the quest for even a single mile more turned into the despair that accompanies the feeling of having come too far to go back, but not far enough to find completion. Despite his inner turmoil, he pressed on and eventually cleared the mountains and pine forests of the northwest and stepped onto the sandy beach of accomplishment, the salty waves of the Pacific Ocean lapping at the soles of his boots.

For me, seeking the Reptilian factor and the connectivity of the serpent in human history and religious myth has been all-consuming, and just when I feel I have fulfilled the goal and step to the ridge of conclusion, there, stretching out before me as far as the eye can see, is another range of snow-capped peaks, each bearing a new rocky climb.

It's the looking for the way through that seems daunting while you are in it. Then, when you finally get there, you look back at the terrain you've traversed and wonder about all the wondrous undiscovered country in other regions extending off to the right or the left of the trail that brought you to this place. Yet, despite all the unexplored territory, you are satisfied that you have at least forged a single path to the other side.

Our ancient past is filled with amazing stories of beings who governed our existence. Whether they were gods descended from the heavens, extraterrestrial beings making their presence known while, perhaps, undergoing their own explorations, or whether they are simply comprised of deified human royal bloodlines and the stuffs of overwrought imaginings and religious control—whichever it may in reality be, they represent the mysterious elements of our past that have comprised the modern mythologies of today. If we take but a moment to stop ourselves in the tracks of our busy work schedules, hang up the phone, shut off the television and the Internet, close the calendar, stop shopping and mowing the grass, and simply "unplug" for a few moments and listen to the quiet, we will find that those voices are still speaking, beckoning us to come find them.

Conclusively answering whether or not extraterrestrial serpentine beings interacted with humanity and continue to make their presence felt from the stealthy shadows is as simplistically easy as finding God sitting on His patio having a cup of Darjeeling. What is certain is that humanity has been writing about these things since they first developed the skill set to record their personal histories. The plethora of occultists, religious apologists, scientists, true believers, skeptics, and experiencers can accomplish only one thing, and that is a presentation of the facts as they understand them. That is why all we are left with, beyond establishing points of history, anthropology, and archaeology—the bare tools of the trade—are the facts, which sometimes controvert the theories.

The things that seem to really matter to the questioning mind, most often never have solid answers. I am again brought to the words of the Richard Fyneman, astralphysicist contemporary of Oppenheimer and Einstein:

> If you expected science could give all the answers to the wonderful questions about "what we are" or "where we're going" or what the meaning of the universe is, and so on, then I think you could easily become disillusioned and then look for some mystic answer to these problems.
>
> …I can live with doubt and uncertainty and not knowing. I think it's much more interesting to live "not knowing" than to have answer which might be wrong. I have approximate

answers and possible beliefs and differing degrees of certainty about different things, but I'm not absolutely sure of anything, and they are many things I don't know anything about. But I don't have to know an answer. I don't feel frightened by not knowing things, about being lost in a mysterious universe without having any purpose.

...I can't believe the special stories that have been made up about our special relationship to the universe...because they seem to be too simple, too connected, too local, too provincial. The earth! He came to the Earth! One of the aspects of God came to the Earth, mind you, and look at what's out there, it isn't in proportion. Anyway, it's no use arguing it...we should look to see what's true and what may not be true. Once you start doubting, which for me is a fundamental part of my soul, to doubt. And ask. And to doubt and ask, it gets a little hard to believe.[1]

Did a race of Reptilians come to this planet long ago? Did extraterrestrials seed the human race or genetically engineer primordial hominids, creating a slave race? Were humans freed from bondage, led by a traitor from the ranks of the alien oppressors? Is there an extraterrestrial race that has sifted in and out of humanity's affairs for all of recorded history, governing our destiny from the shadows? Or are we a race that simply evolves and grows, learning from the past and moving beyond our old superstitions and mythologies? Are we bound by religious thought and man-made myth, only to suffer at its invisible grasp until we move beyond the need for false messiahs and imagined gods, spirits, devils, and monsters that subjugate us to our own fears? Or is it truly that we are the creation of a one, true God, and all the rest is simply the concocted, fabricated veil of lies and deceit, obfuscation and illusion that enslaves us to the dictates of the demonic evil that would stand in the way of our knowing that God in a more real, meaningful way?

These are the questions that I sincerely hope you are left pondering when closing the cover of this book. It is obvious that God does not go out of His way to present His case in a fashion that is not as old, cracked, and crumbling as the last surviving manuscripts telling his story. Accordingly, his opponents seem to work much harder gaining proselytes than He spends attempting to bring us to Him, and so answering the call of religion—even when told it is supposed to be a personal, loving God in charge—is a much more daunting challenge than simply believing things are what they are.

So, toss the coin in the air—or better, roll your 32-sided die. Are we simply creatures at the behest of some greater power, or are a race that lives, thrives and grows off of and in spite of its misty history and scaly mythology? Has humanity experienced the visitations of non-human entities?

Trust no one. Listen to no one. Adhere to no one. Grasp the gift of exploration and seek out the answers for yourself, for if you are comfortable simply living by the dictates of what someone else tells you is so, then you are doomed to live that life of constrained servitude. Think for yourself, and before you know it the answers will make themselves as evident as the nose on your face—the realization that all that remains in the end is a kind of forbidden knowledge, a rage with and beyond reason against reason itself, as exiles from the comforts of bondage, we are composers of a cognitive music that is not a spirituality or a religion, nor is it an eschewing of either, but it is a religion of no religion, a faith of no faith, a belief in no belief.

And, yet, there is that still, small voice…

> "Extinguished theologians lie about the cradle of every
> science, as the strangled snakes beside that of Hercules."
>   —Aldous Huxley

Notes

Chapter 1

1. Glueck, Nelson, *Rivers in the Desert: A History of the Negev: Being an Illustrated Account of Discoveries in a Frontierland of Civilization* (New York: Macmillan; Farrar, Straus & Giroux, 1959), p. 31.

2. Ramsay, William M., *St. Paul the Traveler and the Roman Citizen* (1982), p. 8.

3. Ramsay, William M., *The Bearing of Recent Discovery on the Trustworthiness of the New Testament* (1915), p. 222.

4. Roberts, Scott Alan, *The Rise and Fall of the Nephilim* (Pompton Plains, N.J.: New Page Books, 2012).

5. *Muhammad: Maxime Rodinson,* translated by Anne Carter (1971), pp. 38–49.

6. "Studies on Islam," edited by Merlin L. Swartz, in *Pre-Islamic Bedouin Religion* by Joseph Henninger (1981), pp. 3–22.

7. Muhammad, *The Holy Prophet* (Pakistan: Hafiz Ghulam Sarwar), pp. 18–19.

8. Carlson, Jason, and Ron Carlson, "Why the Secular Left Despise the Christian Right," Christian Ministries International Website, *www. christianministriesintl.org/articles/Why-Secular-Left-Despise-Christian-Right.php.*

9. Heiser, Michael S., PhD, "The Nachash and His Seed: Some Explanatory Notes on Why the 'Serpent' in Genesis 3 Wasn't a Serpent" (Dept. of Hebrew and Semitic Studies, UW-Madison), *www.thedivinecouncil.com/nachashnotes.pdf.*

10. Dalley, Stephanie, *Myths from Mesopotamia: Creation, The Flood, Gilgamesh, and Others* (New York: Oxford University Press, 1989, 2008), pp.13–15.

11. Sitchin, Zechariah, *The Twelfth Planet* (Harper, 2007), Chapter Five: "The Nefilim, People of the Firey Rockets."

12. Heiser, "The Nachash and His Seed."

13. Sitchin, *The Twelfth Planet*, Chapter Five: "The Nefilim, People of the Firey Rockets."

14. Heiser, "The Nachash and His Seed."

15. James, Peter, I. J. Thorpe, Nikos Kokkinos, Robert Morkot, and John Frankish, *Centuries of Darkness: A Challenge to the Conventional Chronology of Old World Archaeology* (London: Jonathan Cape, 1991).

16. Thompson, William Irwin, *Coming into Being: Artifacts and Texts in the Evolution of Consciousness* (Palgrave Macmillan, 1998), pp. 75–76.

17. Roberts, Scott Alan, *The Rise and Fall of the Nephilim* (Psalm 82 and Elohim).

18. Heiser, Michael S., "The Plural Elohim of Psalm 82: Gods or Men?" Michael S. Heiser's Website, *michaelsheiser.com/TheNakedBible/2010/11/the-plural-elohim-of-psalm-82-gods-or-men*, 2010.

19. Dalley, *Myths from Mesopotamia* , pp. 18–19.

20. Pye, Michael, and Kirsten Dalley, *Lost Civilizations and Secrets of the Past* (Pompton Plains, N.J.: New Page Books, 2011), "Cain and the First City."

21. Green, Margaret W. "Eriduu in Sumerian Literature," PhD dissertation, University of Chicato (1975), p. 156: "abzu is often applied to a cosmological region whereas Eridu more precisely designates a geographical site."

22. Lambert, W.G., "Processions to the Akitu House," *Révue d'Assyriologie, RAI 44* (University of Michigan Library, 1997) pp. 75–77.

23. Lawton, Ian, "Guide to Mesopotamian Gods and Pantheons (in Tammuz)," Ian Lawton's Website, *www.ianlawton.com*, 2000.

24. Ibid.

25. Galter, H.D., "Der Gott Ea/Enki in der akkadischen Überlieferung: Eine Bestandsaufnahme des vorhandenen Materials" (Ph.D. diss., Karl-Franzen-Universität Graz., 1983).

26. Halloran, John, *The Sumerian Lexicon, Version 3.0* (Los Angeles, Calif.: Logogram Publishing, 2006), p. 54.

Chapter 2

1. Roberts, Scott Alan, *The Rise and Fall of the Nephilim.*
2. Feynman, Richard, *The Pleasure of Finding Things Out* (Basic Books, 2000).

Chapter 3

1. Kramer, Samuel Noah. *Sumerian Mythology: A Study of Spiritual and Literary Achievement in the Third Millennium BC* (Charleston, S.C.: Forgotten Books, 1997).
2. Malkowski, Edward F., R.A. Schwaller de Lubicz, *The Spiritual Technology of Ancient Egypt: Sacred Science and the Mystery of Consciousness* (Inner Traditions/Bear & Co., 2007), p. 223.
3. Her Holiness Shri Mataji Nirmala Devi Srivastava, *Meta Modern Era* (Vishwa Nirmala Dharma, first edition, 1995), pp. 233–248.
4. Barton, Stephen C., and David Wilkinson, *Reading Genesis After Darwin ("Midrash, Rabba to Genesis")* (New York: Oxford University Press, 2009), p. 93.
5. Loud, Gordon, *Megiddo II,* Plates 240:1, 4. The serpents came from Stratum X (dated 1650–1550 BCE) and Stratum VIIB (dated 1150–1250 BCE) and cannot definitely be associated with the cult.
6. Macalister, R.A.S., *Gezer II,* p. 399, fig. 488. The serpent came from the high place area and apparently is to be dated in the Late Bronze Age.
7. Yadin et al., *Hazor III–IV,* Plates, pl. 339: 5–6. The serpents are from Stratum I (Late Bronze Age II). Yadin informs of their provenance in a personal correspondence.
8. Ringle, William M., Tomás Gallareta Negrón, and George J. Bey, "The Return of Quetzalcoatl" in *Ancient Mesoamerica* (Cambridge University Press, 1998), pp. 183–232.
9. Smith, Michael E., *The Aztecs (2nd edition)* (Malden, Mass.: Blackwell Publishing, 2001), p. 213.
10. Hancock, Graham, *Fingerprints of the Gods: The Evidence of Earth's Lost Civilization (1st Edition)* (Crown, 1995).
11. *Pliny the Elder,* eds. John Bostock and H.T. Riley (translators), "The Natural History." 1855. viii. 33.
12. This list comes from *wyrddin.com.*
13. Bickel, Susanne, "Apophis" in *Iconography of Deities and Demons in the Ancient Near East.* Electronic pre-publication revision, November 20, 2007, accessed at *www.religionswissenschaft.unizh.ch/idd/prepublications/e_idd_apophis.pdf.*

14. Moscati, Sabatino, *The Face of the Ancient Orient* (Garden City, N.Y.: Doubleday Anchor Books, 1962), pp. 125–127.

15. Frankfort, Henri, *Kingship and the Gods* (Chicago, Ill.: The University of Chicago Press, 1962), pp. 145–146.

16. Lurker, Manfred. *Gods and Symbols of Ancient Egypt,* (London: Thames and Hudson, 1984), pp. 26, 10.

17. Frankfort, *Kingship and the Gods,* p. 180.

18. Lurker, *Gods and Symbols of Ancient Egypt,* 108.

19. Moscati, Sabatino, *The Face of the Ancient Orient,* pp. 125–26; and Lurker, *Gods and Symbols of Ancient Egypt,* p. 93.

20. Lurker, Manfred, "Snakes," in *The Encyclopedia of Religion* (New York: Macmillan, 1987), 13:373.

21. Joines, Karen R., *Serpent Symbolism in the Old Testament: A Linguistic, Archaeological, and Literary Study* (Haddonfield, N.J.: Haddonfield House, 1974), p. 19.

22. Lurker, *Gods and Symbols of Ancient Egypt,* p. 108.

23. Frankfort, Henri, *Kingship and the Gods,* p. 119.

24. Franklin, Benjamin, *Pennsylvania Journal* (December 27, 1775).

Chapter 4

1. Milliren, Alan P. "Adlerian Theory." Available at *www.carterandevans.com/portal/index.php/adlerian-theory/69-adlerian-theory.*

2. Aristotle, *Physics* 194 b17–20. See also: *Posterior Analytics* 71 b9–11; 94 a20.

3. Horney, Karen, *Self-Analysis* (New York: Norton & Company Inc., 1942).

4. "Reptilians," Wikipedia, *en.wikipedia.org/wiki/Reptilians.*

5. "Reptilians," Crystalinks Metaphysics and Science Website, *www.crystalinks.com/reptilians.html.*

6. "The Reptilians: Who Are They Really?" Dreams of the Great Earthchanges Website, *www.greatdreams.com/reptlan/reps.htm.*

7. "Alien Nation," The Watcher Files Website, *www.thewatcherfiles.com/exposing_reptilians.htm.*

8. Rhodes, John, "The Reptilian-Human Connection," Reptoids.com, *www.reptoids.com/Vault/ArticleClassics/1994RepHuConn.htm.*

9. "The Reptilians," The Nibiruan Council Website, *www.nibiruancouncil.com/html/reptilians.html.*

10. "Reptilian Agenda," David Icke's Website, *www.davidicke.com/articles/reptilian-agenda-mainmenu-43.*

11. "The Occult Reptilian Sage," Biblioteca Pleyades Website, *www. bibliotecapleyades.net/sumer_anunnaki/reptiles/reptiles.htm.*
12. "The Reptilians," Whale Website, *www.whale.to/b/reptilian_h.html.*
13. Rhodes, John, "The Reptilian-Human Connection."
14. Russell, D.A. "Speculations on the Evolution of Intelligence in Multicellular Organisms." CP-2156, Life in the Universe Conference.
15. "Alex Collier: On Reptilians: The Draconians and the Paa Tal," Biblioteca Pleyades Website, *www.bibliotecapleyades.net/sumer_anunnaki/reptiles/ reptiles33.htm#The%20Draconians%20and%20the%20Paa%20Tal.*
16. Hecht, Jeff, *Cosmos Magazine 315* (June 2007). This article highlights the hypothesis of Dale Russell's dinosauroid.
17. Russell, Dale, and Wallace Tucker, "Supernovae and the Extinction of the Dinosaurs," *Nature 229* (Fenruary 1971), 553–554.

Chapter 5
1. Gibson, David J. "The Land of Eden Located," Unpublished manuscript, available at *nabataea.net/eden.html.*
2. Taylor, Bernard A., *Analytical Lexicon to the Septuagint* (Peabody, Mass.: Hendrickson Publishers, expanded edition, 2009).
3. Silva, Moisés, and Karen H. Jobes, *Invitation to the Septuagint* (Grand Rapids, Mich.: Baker Academic, 2005).

Chapter 6
1. Geary, Patrick J., *Before France and Germany: The Creation and Transformation of the Merovingian World* (New York: Oxford University Press, 1988).
2. Knight, Xharles, T*he English Cyclopaedia: Volume IV* (London: Nabu Press, 2010), p. 733.
3. Rendina, Claudio, and Paul McCusker, *The Popes: Histories and Secrets* (New York: Seven Locks Press, 2002), p. 145.
4. Baigent, Michael, Richard Leigh, and Henry Lincoln, *The Holy Blood and the Holy Grail: The Secret History of Jesus and the Shocking Legacy of the Grail* (New York: Delacorte Press, 1982).
5. Burgess, Anthony, *But Do Blondes Prefer Gentlemen Homage to Qwert Yuiop and Other Writings* (New York: McGraw-Hill, 1986), pp. 33–35.
6. Gardner, Laurence, *Bloodline of the Holy Grail: The Hidden Lineage of Jesus Revealed* (Lions Bay, British Columbia, Canada: Fair Winds Press, 2002).

7. Gardner, Laurence, *Genesis of the Grail Kings: The Explosive Story of Genetic Cloning and the Ancient Bloodline of Jesus* (Lions Bay, British Columbia, Canada: Fair Winds Press, 2002).

8. Hopkins, Marilyn, Graham Simmans, and Tim Wallace-Murphy, *Rex Deus: The True Mystery of Rennes-Le-Chateau* (Shaftesbury, Dorset, UK: Element Books, 2000).

9. Haskins, Susan, *Mary Magdalen: The Essential History* (London: Pimlico, 2003), p. 96.

10. Evans, Craig A., *Fabricating Jesus: How Modern Scholars Distort the Gospels* (Downers Grove, Ill.: Ivp Books, 2008), p. 94.

11. Pseudo-Fredegar, "Historia" in *Monumenta Germaniae Historica, Scriptores Rerum Merovingicarum, Tomus II* (Hannover Press, 1888).

12. Ellis, Peter Berresford, *The Mammoth Book of Celtic Myths and Legends* (London: Constable & Robinson, 2002), p. 28.

13. *Dictionary of the Irish Language, Compact Edition* (Dublin, Ireland: Royal Irish Academy, 1990), p. 612.

14. MacKillop, James, *Dictionary of Celtic Mythology* (New York: Oxford University Press), p. 366.

15. *Lebor Gabála Érenn: Book of the Taking of Ireland Part 1-5.* Edited and translated by R.A.S. Macalister. (Dublin, Ireland: Irish Texts Society, 1941.)

16. Ibid.

17. Gardner, Sir Laurence, *Realm of the Ring Lords: The Myth and Magic of the Grail Quest* (Lions Bay, British Columbia, Canada: Fair Winds Press, 2003).

18. Aho, Barbara, "The Merovingian Dynasty," Watch Unto Prayer Website, *watch.pair.com/merovingian.html.*

19. Van Buren, Elizabeth, *The Sign of the Dove* (Suffolk, UK: Neville Spearman, Ltd., 1983), pp. 141–142.

20. Ibid.

21. Franke, Sylvia, *Tree of Life and The Holy Grail: Ancient and Modern Spiritual Paths and the Mystery of Rennes-le-chateau* (ZEast Sussex, UK: Temple Lodge Publishing, 2007), p. 127.

22. Patai, Raphael, *The Hebrew Goddess* (New York: Ktav Publishing House, 1967).

23. Blunt, John Henry, *Dictionary of Sects, Heresies, Ecclesiastical Parties, and Schools of Religious Thought* (Rivingtons, 1874), p. 95.

24. Mead, G.R.S., *Fragments of a Faith Forgotten* (Whitefish, Mont.: Kessinger Publishing LLC, 1992), p. 225.

25. Blunt, John Henry, *Dictionary of Sects, Heresies, Ecclesiastical Parties, and Schools of Religious Thought* (Rivingtons, 1874), p. 95.

26. *Biblia Sacra Vulgata*, Exodus 34:29–35.

27. Phelps, Reginald H., "Before Hitler Came: Thule Society and Germanen Orden," *Journal of Modern History* (University of Chicago Press, 1963), pp. 245–261.

28. Goodrick-Clarke, Nicholas, *The Occult Roots of Nazism: The Ariosophists of Austria and Germany 1890–1935* (Wellingborough, England: The Aquarian Press, 1985, republished 1992).

29. Daim, Wilfried, *Der Mann, der Hitler die Ideen gab (The Man, Who Gave Hitler the Ideas)* (1958).

30. Kershaw, Ian, *Hitler: 1889–1936 Hubris* (New York: W.W. Norton & Company, 2000), pp. 138–139.

31. Bromer, Dietrich, *Bevor Hitler kam: Eine historische Studie* (Marva Publishing, Aulf Edition, 1933, 1972), p. 42.

32. Goodrick-Clarke, Nicholas, *The Occult Roots of Nazism: The Ariosophists of Austria and Germany 1890–1935* (Wellingborough, England: The Aquarian Press, 1985, republished 1992), pp. 127–128.

33. Strohm, Harald, *Die Gnosis und der Nationalsozialismus (Gnosis and National Socialism)* (Berlin, Germany: Suhrkamp, 1973).

34. Abrams, Kevin, and Scott Lively, *The Pink Swastiks: Homesexuality in the Nazi Party* (Founders Publishing Corp., 1995).

35. Goodrick-Clarke, Nicholas, *The Occult Roots of Nazism* , pp. 131, 142.

36. "The Merovingian Infiltration of the Christian World Through Monasticism," *www.angelfire.com/journal2/post/infiltration.html.*

37. Blavatsky, H.P., *The Secret Doctrine (abridged & annotated edition)* (New York: Tarcher (Penguin), 2009).

Chapter 7

1. Easwaran, Eknath, *A Glossary of Sanskrit from the Spiritual Tradition of India* (Berkeley, Calif.: Blue Mountain Center of Meditation, 1970), p. 5.

2. Header of David Icke's Website. *www.davidicke.com.*

3. Ibid.

4. In Icke's own words at *www.amazon.com/wiki/David_Icke/ref=ntt_at_bio_wiki.*

5. Icke, David, "List of Famous Satanists, Pedophiles, and Mind Controllers." The Forbidden Knowledge Website. *www.theforbiddenknowledge.com/hardtruth/list_of_satanist.htm.*

6. Icke, David, *Children of the Matrix,* p. 291ff; and David Icke, *The Biggest Secret,* pp. 30–40.

7. "Reptilians, Reptilian Aliens." *Arcturi.com, arcturi.com/ReptilianArchives. html.*

8. Icke, David, *In the Light of Experience* (Time Warner Paperbacks, 1993), pp. 190, 208.

9. Ibid., p. 193.

10. Icke, David, *Children of the Matrix,* pp. 30–40.

11. David Icke's Website, *www.davidicke.com/articles/reptilian-agenda-mainmenu-43.*

Afterword

1. Feynman, Richard, *The Pleasure of Finding Things Out.*

Index

About the Author

Scott Alan Roberts is the founder and publisher of *INTREPID Magazine* (*www.intrepidmag.com*), a publication that boasts an eclectic focus on science, politics, culture, ancient civilizations, conspiracies, ancient aliens, and unexplained phenomena.

Roberts is an accomplished illustrator and writer of fiction and non-fiction. He can be more or less defined by his roles as Dad and Husband, and is a parent to five exuberant children, three of whom are still young enough to live at home. These ingredients combined have made Roberts's life a paradoxical roller coaster of hellacious joy and insightful befuddlement, and were it not for his self-acclaimed buoyant, easy-going nature, he insists he would most assuredly have lost his sanity a long time ago.

Having spent the bulk of the last 25 years in advertising as a creative director, designer, and illustrator, Roberts's background is laced with varied and diverse skills and experience in publishing and marketing. He possesses an astute flare for the visually dramatic, demonstrated in his various ventures from theatre to comic book art and publishing, as well as advertising campaigns and public speaking.

After two years in a Christian bible college, he entered seminary, pursuing his Masters in Divinity (Mdiv) and worked as a youth director alongside his advertising career. His religious studies intensified his natural interest in spirituality, and his research of the paranormal expanded throughout the following years, much to the chagrin of many of his former Bible school fellows.

Shortly after his seminary years, Roberts began a small comic book publishing effort, writing and illustrating stories, which were also pitched as animated television series. He developed and published *The Bloodlore Chronicles,* as well as the highly successful *Ancient Heroes* trading card series, and began development on a series of chapter books. He authored and illustrated his first historical teen novel, *The Rollicking Adventures of Tam O'Hare (www.tamohare.com),* which garnered success in the teen and college markets in 2008 and 2009.

Roberts began his delve into paranormal investigation in 1999 by co-hosting and producing Three Horizons Paranormal Radio airing in Oklahoma City and several affiliates. He simultaneously launched a fledgling paranormal investigative long before the pop culture of paranormal investigation was "all the rage."

Roberts's current projects include *Tam O'Hare and the Banshee of BallyGlenMorrow,* the second in his series of Tam O'Hare historical novels, and a more scholarly effort on the historical Moses, tentatively entitled *The Grimoire of Moses: An Historical Exploration of the Majick and Mysticism Behind The Great Exodus and Its Enigmatic Leader,* co-authored with archaeologist/anthropologist Dr. John Ward. He is also working on a joint authoring effort with *INTREPID Magazine* partner Micah Hanks, *At Odds: The Pervasive, Perpetual Conflict Between Science and Religion.*

Roberts is a standup philosopher, and frequent guest speaker at many conferences and events around the country and abroad. He is the former Editor-In-Chief of *TAPS ParaMagazine,* the official publication of SyFy's *Ghost Hunters.*

Roberts currently lives with his family not far from the Minneapolis/Saint Paul metro area, where he grew up and lived most of his life. You can see more visiting his Website (*www.scottalanroberts.com*).